THE CONDITIONS

OF

OUR LORD'S LIFE ON EARTH

THE BISHOP PADDOCK LECTURES, 1896

THE CONDITIONS

OF

OUR LORD'S LIFE ON EARTH

Being Five Lectures delivered on the Bishop Paddock
Foundation, in the General Seminary at New York, 1896

TO WHICH IS PREFIXED PART OF A
FIRST PROFESSORIAL LECTURE AT CAMBRIDGE

BY

ARTHUR JAMES MASON, D.D.

LADY MARGARET PROFESSOR OF DIVINITY AND FELLOW OF JESUS COLLEGE
CAMBRIDGE; CANON OF ST. SAVIOUR'S, CANTERBURY

WIPF & STOCK · Eugene, Oregon

Wipf and Stock Publishers
199 W 8th Ave, Suite 3
Eugene, OR 97401

The Conditions of Our Lord's Life on Earth
Being Five Lectures delivered on the Bishop Paddock Foundation,
in the General Seminary at New York, 1896: To Which is Prefixed
Part of a First Professorial Lecture at Cambridge
By Mason, Arthur James
Softcover ISBN-13: 978-1-6667-6166-5
Hardcover ISBN-13: 978-1-6667-6167-2
eBook ISBN-13: 978-1-6667-6168-9
Publication date 10/10/2022
Previously published by Longmans, Green, & Co., 1896

This edition is a scanned facsimile of
the original edition published in 1896.

TO THE VERY REVEREND
FREDERICK WILLIAM FARRAR, D.D.,
DEAN OF CANTERBURY,
WHOSE NAME IS EVERYWHERE ASSOCIATED WITH
THE LIFE OF CHRIST,
THIS LITTLE VOLUME IS DEDICATED
BY ONE WHO HAS HAD FOR A YEAR THE PRIVILEGE OF
WORKING UNDER HIM,
AND HAS RECEIVED GREAT KINDNESSES AT HIS HANDS.

THE BISHOP PADDOCK LECTURES.

In the summer of the year 1880, George A. Jarvis of Brooklyn, New York, moved by his sense of the great good which might thereby accrue to the cause of Christ, and to the Church of which he was an ever-grateful member, gave to the General Theological Seminary of the Protestant Episcopal Church certain securities, exceeding in value eleven thousand dollars, for the foundation and maintenance of a Lectureship in said seminary.

Out of love to a former pastor and enduring friend, the Right Reverend Benjamin Henry Paddock, D.D., Bishop of Massachusetts, he named the foundation "The Bishop Paddock Lectureship."

The deed of trust declares that "*the subjects of the lectures shall be such as appertain to the* defence of the religion of Jesus Christ, as revealed in the *Holy Bible*, and illustrated in the *Book of Common Prayer*, against the varying errors of the day, whether materialistic, rationalistic, or professedly religious, and also to its defence and confirmation in respect of such central truths as the *Trinity*, the *Atonement, Justification*, and the *Inspiration of the Word of God;* and of such central facts as the *Church's Divine Order and Sacraments*, her historical *Reformation*, and her rights and powers as a pure and national Church. *And* other subjects may be chosen if unanimously approved by the Board of Appointment as being both timely and also within the true intent of this Lectureship."

Under the appointment of the Board created by the trust, the Rev. Arthur James Mason, D.D., Canon of Canterbury, and Lady Margaret Professor of Divinity in the University of Cambridge, delivered the Lectures for the year 1896, contained in this volume.

PREFACE

THE last three of these Lectures were in substance delivered to the clergy of Worcester and the neighbourhood, in the chapter-house of that Cathedral, in 1892 and 1895, and to the summer gathering of clergy at Cambridge in 1894.

When the Trustees of the Paddock Lecture Fund did me the honour to invite me to lecture on that foundation, I thought I could do no better than take the same subject, feeling that a reverent treatment of it would tend more than anything else to draw out the personal devotion of the students of the General Seminary towards our Blessed Saviour, whose ministers they were about to become, and that a full examination of the Scriptural data might tend to modify impressions which recent criticism upon our Lord's use of the Old Testament was tending to create. I wish, however, to make it plain that the authorities of the Seminary were in no way responsible for my manner of dealing with the subject. Amidst the utmost kindness and courtesy, which I shall remember as long as I live, it became apparent to me, before the Lectures were at an end, that what I had been led to say did not meet with unmixed approval. I cannot but hope that some of the misgivings which the Lectures aroused may be removed by the perusal of them in print. It is one thing to listen to spoken words, perhaps under conditions not very favourable to accurate hearing, and another thing to look at them quietly in the study. One American newspaper which has been forwarded to me, speaks as if there were some uncertainty as to whether I believed in the Godhead of Christ or not. Such an insinuation would have been totally impossible on the part of any one who had heard me. The Godhead of Christ is not only explicitly and in set terms asserted in many passages of the New Testament; it forms the substratum of the entire Bible, and of all history. Without the Godhead of Christ the Bible would be a self-contradictory chaos, and the history of man and of the world would be meaningless.

A more acute and serious criticism was directed against my third lecture, so I am informed, by a respected English priest, who has given himself to the service of a parish in the American Church. He considered that my treatment of our Lord's miracles (of which he was only able to judge by report) came under the ninth Anathema of Cyril, which, along with the other eleven Anathemas, was adopted by the Ecumenical Council of Ephesus, and reaffirmed by later Councils. That Anathema runs thus:—

"If any man saith that the one Lord Jesus Christ was glorified by the Spirit, and used the power that came by Him as a power that was not His own, and received from Him the ability to work miracles against unclean spirits and to perform Divine signs among men, instead of saying that the Spirit through whom He wrought the signs was His own Spirit, let him be Anathema."[1]

---

[1] I translate the text as given in P. E. Pusey's *Cyril* vol. vi. pp. 36 and 254: Εἴ τις φησὶ τὸν ἕνα Κύριον Ἰησοῦν Χριστὸν

It must be remembered, however, what was the special heresy against which the Anathemas of Cyril were directed. The word "one," near the beginning of the ninth, strikes the note. They are directed against Nestorianism, not against Arianism, or any form of thought which might seem to lower the eternal Person of the Word as such. The Nestorian heresy made the Lord Jesus Christ two persons, not one; and it would seem (we know little of Nestorius's teaching except through Cyril's polemic against it) that Nestorius had used the text, "He shall glorify Me" (St. John xvi. 14), as an indication that there was in Christ a human person who could speak of being glorified by the Spirit, distinct from that Divine Person of the Word who,

---

δεδοξάσθαι παρὰ τοῦ πνεύματος, ὡς ἀλλοτρίᾳ δυνάμει τῇ δι' αὐτοῦ χρώμενον, καὶ παρ' αὐτοῦ λαβόντα τὸ ἐνεργεῖν δύνασθαι κατὰ πνευμάτων ἀκαθάρτων, καὶ τὸ πληροῦν εἰς ἀνθρώπους τὰς θεοσημίας, καὶ οὐχὶ δὴ μᾶλλον ἴδιον αὐτοῦ τὸ πνεῦμά φησι, δι' οὗ καὶ ἐνήργηκε τὰς θεοσημίας, ἀνάθεμα ἔστω. Aubert's text reads: Τῇ ἰδίᾳ αὐτοῦ for τῇ δι' αὐτοῦ; and so does Theodoret, according to the Paris text of 1642. This would yield the sense, "and used the power which was, in fact, His own, as though it were another's." The Anathemas may be found also in Labbe's *Councils* vol. iii. p. 410, or in a handy form in Denzinger's *Enchiridion Symbolorum et Definitionum* p. 23.

it was assumed, could not be so glorified. It seems to have been further assumed[1] that the form in which the Spirit thus glorified the human person associated with the Word, was the working of miracles by Jesus Himself, including the Ascension, or by His disciples afterwards.

The "explanation" of this Anathema, which was given by Cyril himself to the Council of Ephesus, was as follows: "The only begotten Word of God, when He was made Man, remained God also, being all things that the Father is, except only the Fatherhood; and He wrought the Divine signs, having as His own the Holy Spirit, who is from Him and essentially is in Him ($\tau\grave{o}$ $\dot{\epsilon}\xi$ $\alpha\dot{v}\tau o\hat{v}$ $\kappa\alpha\grave{\iota}$ $o\dot{v}\sigma\iota\omega\delta\hat{\omega}\varsigma$ $\dot{\epsilon}\mu\pi\epsilon\phi\upsilon\kappa\grave{o}\varsigma$ $\alpha\dot{v}\tau\hat{\wp}$); so that, though He was become Man, yet, because He remained God also, He performed the miracles as by His own power when He performed them by the power of the Spirit. Those who say that He was glorified by the operation of the Spirit after the fashion of an ordinary man, or of one of the saints, which He employed, not as His own, but as that of another

[1] See Pusey's *Cyril* vi. p. 32.

who was Divine (ὡς ἀλλοτρίᾳ καὶ θεοπρεπεῖ), and that He received from the Spirit as a gift of grace His Ascension into heaven, will justly lie under the force of the Anathema."[1]

It was an unwarranted assumption when (as it appears) on either side it was supposed that "to glorify," in the sense of St. John's Gospel, must imply an increase of glory, which could not properly be predicated of a Divine person. "To glorify Christ" can be as truly said as "to glorify God," which is so frequent an expression in the Bible. Neither was it by the miracles only, nor even chiefly, whether before or after the Ascension, that the Spirit is said to glorify Christ; it was by displaying on a much larger scale, as well as in a much more inward and penetrating fashion, the majesty of the co-equal Son. Cyril's exegesis in this matter was not much better, perhaps, than that of Nestorius. But with regard to his main point, he was unquestionably right. Whatever further difficulty of interpretation might be involved, Jesus Christ was one, not two; He was the

[1] Pusey's *Cyril* vi. p. 254.

Divine Word, made man, yet remaining very God; and when He said that the Spirit should glorify Him, it was He Himself, the Incarnate Word, who said it, 'and not a human person caught up into a peculiar relation with Him— nor, for that matter, a human nature, as Theodoret would have made out;[1] and whatever that glorifying might consist of, the Spirit who was to perform it was essentially His own Spirit, proceeding from Himself as well as from the Father, and dwelling in Him as well as in the Father. The Anathema was justly in force against those who conceived otherwise.

The view which is suggested in my lecture, as resulting from the juxtaposition of all the Scripture passages bearing on the subject, is one which does not appear to have entered into the mind of either Nestorius or Cyril, and which, therefore, is altogether outside the scope of Cyril's censure. It is that the Eternal Son Himself, from whom the Holy Ghost proceeds, vouchsafed to take the position of a recipient of the Holy Ghost, and, although He might

[1] Theodoret *Repr. XII. Capitum Cyrilli.*

at every moment have worked His wonderful works by His own intrinsic Divine power, chose to work them rather by what may be called the power of another,—though the power of that other was throughout, in Cyril's sense, His own. There is no derogation from the perfection of Christ's Godhead if, according to what appears to be the natural meaning of the New Testament words, we suppose our Lord to have voluntarily assumed, and consistently maintained upon earth, a position which was not that to which His Divine nature entitled Him, and which He might at any instant have abandoned, had He so willed.

Cyril's Anathema, then, is not directed against a view in the smallest degree resembling that which is advanced in these lectures. But it may be acknowledged, all the same, that the *animus* of Cyril's theology in general is opposed to the line here taken. It is well known that St. Cyril, though it is unjust to charge him with Eutychianism or Monophysitism, yet lays himself open to the charge of minimizing the significance of our Lord's Humanity. Had he been more sensitive to the consecrated language of Scripture with regard to our Lord's Humanity, he would have been a more successful opponent of Nestorianism.[1]

The fact is, that ancient theologians, Catholic and heretical alike,—and the same thing holds true of many modern ones,—did not altogether form their systems upon a scientific and methodical examination of the words of Holy Scripture. It was not at all that they thought lightly of the authority of Holy Scripture, or consciously set some other source of doctrine over against it; their arguments are almost wholly of an exegetical and Scriptural kind. But their minds were often preoccupied by ideas (sometimes not of purely Christian origin) with regard to what the Divine nature must needs be, which occasionally led them into ways of interpretation which were not the simplest and most natural.

The providence of God has guarded the Church from making or accepting any pronouncement

---

[1] The attitude of Cyril is well described in Dorner's *Doctrine of the Person of Christ* (Engl. Tr.) Div. II. vol. i. p. 65, foll.; and there is a good catena of passages from him in Bruce's *Humiliation of Christ* p. 366, foll.; comp. p. 50, foll.

upon the relation of the Two Natures of Christ which would be at all in conflict with Holy Scripture. However strongly the tide may at times have run in the direction opposed to a full belief in our Lord's Humanity, the way is left open for this side of the doctrine of the Incarnation to be developed by men who hold firmly the Catholic teaching concerning His essential and absolute Godhead. In such a development, Holy Scripture must be, not merely the supreme arbiter, but the ground, and the fountain, and the material, and the all in all. We need, in many things, not only to take salient texts and interpret them by themselves, but to endeavour to work all through Scripture and collect everything that bears upon the point under investigation, and dispassionately to see what conclusion may issue from such exhaustive comparisons. The following Lectures are an attempt, however ill-executed it may be, to contribute to such a New Testament Theology. With reference to our Saviour's miracles in particular, I could wish that the very plain words of St. Peter, in Acts x. 38, might be taken as a standard, and other passages of Scripture ranged either beside it, or on the opposite side, if there are any which put forward a different aspect. I do not know of any to set on the opposite side ; and if there should ever be found to be a discrepancy between the language of St. Cyril and that of St. Peter (or St. Luke), I suppose we should all, without hesitation, adopt the latter.

I have somewhat purposely abstained from reading modern works upon the κένωσις of the Son of God, not wishing my study of the New Testament teaching upon the subject to be more indebted than was necessary to secondary sources. I have read the historical part of Dr. Bruce's *Humiliation of Christ;* but I have not read Mr. Gore's *Bampton Lectures* or *Dissertations on Subjects connected with the Incarnation,* nor Mr. Swayne's on the *Human Knowledge of our Lord.*

Since my return from America, the Bishop of Edinburgh has very kindly pointed out to me, through a friend, a most valuable Charge by the late Bishop (O'Brien) of Ossory, in which much the same kind of line is taken as in these Lectures. The Charge was a reply to the crude and almost Socinian theories which had then been recently put forth by Bishop Colenso. It would have been well if all the replies to Colenso had been marked by the same dignity, and the same reasonableness, and the same readiness to see what the Scriptures have really to say upon the points under consideration, as that part of Bishop O'Brien's Charge with which we are at present concerned. From it I would quote the following words:—

"Some think . . . that we cannot adopt any interpretation of the Lord's words which would represent Him as having undergone anything beyond an outward or relative change in taking our nature. From the impossibility of conceiving any change in the Infinite, they seem to have inferred, if they did not confound the two things, that any such change is impossible. But, however safely we may hold that it is impossible that any such change can take place through any other agency, it would seem very rash and presumptuous to deny the possibility of its being effected by the will of the Infinite Being Himself. I should say this, supposing that we had no way of arriving at any conclusion on the question but the high *priori* road. But we have a much safer, though a humbler way. . . . Where the Infinite is concerned, we can rely but little upon any collection of our own reason, unless it be confirmed by Revelation. Here, however, there is no want of such confirmation, nor can we, I think, read the Holy Scriptures fairly without finding it."[1]

I must repeat again, what I have said more than once in the Lectures themselves, that it has not been my intention to put forward a complete theory of the position assumed by our Lord upon earth, but only to bring together the material out of which any Scriptural theory of it must be formed. There is probably much material that I have overlooked, and there are, no doubt, other ways both of interpreting and of arranging the material which I

---

[1] *A Charge delivered to the Clergy of the United Dioceses of Ossory, Ferns, and Leighlin, at his Ordinary Visitation in October*, 1863, *by J. T. O'Brien, D.D.* (Macmillan), p. 104.

have collected; but I trust that nothing which I have said will, on inspection, be found incompatible with fidelity to that doctrine of the Person of Christ which was once for all declared for us by the labours of the Fathers of the four great Councils.

I have ventured to prefix to the Paddock Lectures part of my Introductory Lecture as Lady Margaret Professor at Cambridge, delivered in January last, as urging somewhat more fully what I believe to be one of the chief requirements of the time, and indeed of all times,—the continued re-investigation of the New Testament for the purposes of Dogmatic Theology.

CANTERBURY,
　　July, 1896.

CONTENTS

	PAGE
PART OF INTRODUCTORY LECTURE AT CAMBRIDGE	1

LECTURE I.

THE HISTORICAL METHOD OF STUDYING OUR LORD'S LIFE UPON EARTH 26

LECTURE II.

THE DEVELOPMENT OF OUR LORD'S MORAL CHARACTER AS MAN. 51

LECTURE III.

OUR LORD'S POWER UPON EARTH 84

LECTURE IV.

OUR LORD'S KNOWLEDGE UPON EARTH—APPEARANCES OF LIMITATION 114

LECTURE V.

OUR LORD'S KNOWLEDGE UPON EARTH—ITS TRANSCENDENCE 155

PART OF INTRODUCTORY LECTURE AT CAMBRIDGE.

*   *   *   *

IT has been the fashion in some quarters to assert, and to assert sometimes with a good deal of asperity, that Cambridge has done little for Dogmatic Theology. The complaint cannot, of course, be lodged against the Cambridge of former days—I will not say of the days of Overall and Pearson, nor even of the days of Waterland. The charge could not justly be made in the days of Mill, whose *Five Sermons on the Temptation of Christ*, not to mention other works of his, are, I venture to think, as fine a piece of doctrinal exposition as could well be named. But coming to the days which I, at any rate, know best, is it really the case that Cambridge has been behindhand in definite teaching of the contents of the Christian faith? I will not speak of what has been done by means of the *history* of doctrine, though it is impossible to read treatises like Dr. Hort's on the history of the words ΜΟΝΟΓΕΝΗС ΘΕΟС, or (if I may name one who is now here) Dr. Swete's on the history of the doctrine of the Procession of the Holy Spirit, without gaining the clearest guidance on high points of theology. In direct statement, very great help to the students of Dogmatics has been given in recent years at Cambridge. It would not have been possible for any Schoolman of the Middle Ages to lay out a more comprehensive, or at the same time a more subtle and delicate, scheme of Christian Dogmatics than that which was laid out by Dr. Westcott, in courses of lectures which I attended as a Bachelor of Arts, and which were, I believe, repeated several times afterwards. And I cannot think where a man might hopefully turn, when wishing for an exact presentation of the orthodox teaching with regard to the

Person of Christ, if he fails to find it in such notes as Dr. Lightfoot's upon the Πρωτότοκος of the Epistle to the Colossians, or Dr. Westcott's upon the cardinal passages of St. John and of the Epistle to the Hebrews.

Dogmatic theology has, perhaps, not been obtruded upon students here; and I have little doubt that most of us would be unfeignedly sorry if it had been. Few sober-minded people have not at some time or other been plagued and wounded by the peremptory young man, primed with other men's formulæ, or with his own version of them, who has little experience of the labour which has evolved them, and no reserve in the enuntiation of them. Theology is not the only subject in which such rough dogmatism is possible. Happily that is not the type which has generally been developed by the Cambridge Schools. Respect for the healthy growth of young men's minds demands a different treatment. We have no wish here to substitute authority for conviction. We have not been accustomed to purvey for men opinions ready made in any department of knowledge, least of all in that which is of the highest importance. That was not, as a Cambridge pen has shown, the mode of education adopted by the *Pastor Pastorum ;* and, indeed, it would not be education at all. Full, accurate, Catholic doctrinal teaching has, no one can deny it, been diligently and continuously given at Cambridge ; but it has been given chiefly in the forms that are most like life, in the history of Christian thought, and in the interpretation of the Christian Scriptures.

For the English Churchman there can be no doubt where to look for the doctrine which he is to teach and to receive. It is not an undervaluing of Ecclesiastical Tradition to say that the one perennial fountain of Christian doctrine is in the Bible. Tradition, in the case of a great historical and still living corporation, is, of course, of first-rate importance. To an openeyed observer, a few weeks of practical intercourse with the men who hold a religion conveys more notion of what that religion is than a year's study of its books. Yet there are many reasons why tradition cannot be regarded by a free-minded Christian as a co-ordinate source of doctrine along with Scripture.

In the first place, it will, I think, be almost invariably found that where the Fathers, as they frequently do, insist upon the importance of traditions as distinct from Scriptures, the traditions upon which they are insisting are traditions relating to practice, and only indirectly to doctrine. To disregard Church tradition was to them the mark of a heretic; but the traditions which they claim to have received from Apostolic days, apart from the written Word, were usages and observances, ceremonies and rites. Thus, in a famous passage, Tertullian argues, "We make offerings for the dead, and on the anniversary of the martyrs' birthdays; we count it wrong to fast or to kneel for prayer upon the Lord's day. We enjoy the same freedom from Easter Day to Pentecost. We are much distressed if any portion of wine or bread, though it be but our own wine or bread, fall to the ground. At every movement . . . we rub the sign of the cross upon our brows. Ask as you may, you will find no law of the Scriptures which prescribes these and similar compliances. You will be informed that tradition prescribes, custom ratifies, and faith observes them."[1] Or again, in another well-known passage, Basil says, "Some of the things agreed upon and taught in the Church are gathered from the written instruction; others we have received as a sacred secret by tradition from the Apostles. Both these classes are of equal religious importance. No one will deny it—at any rate, no one who has the slightest acquaintance with ecclesiastical institutions." But the instances which he goes on to give are such as these: "Who ever taught in writing that those who have hoped in the Name of our Lord Jesus Christ (*i.e.* catechumens) should be marked with the sign of the cross? What writing taught us to turn to the east in praying? . . . We bless the baptismal water, the anointing oil, the candidate for Baptism himself,—on what written authority? Is it not from the silent and secret tradition?"[2] He says much more to the same point.

I do not know of one article of belief which

[1] Tert. *de Corona* §§ 3, 4.   [2] Bas. *de Spiritu Sancto* §§ 27.

is asserted by the Fathers to be derived from tradition outside of the canon of Scripture. Franzelin, the chief modern exponent of the Roman theory of tradition, only attempts to name two—that infants are to be baptized, and that the Bible is an inspired whole. But there is no doctrine of Infant Baptism as distinct from Baptism in general, however it may suit Jesuit and Baptist to affirm that there is; and the doctrine of Baptism is quite sufficiently set forth in Scripture for all purposes. Nor would it be easy to say what Catholic doctrine concerning the inspiration of the Bible has come down to us by tradition without being witnessed to in the Bible itself. The inspiration of the New Testament is neither more nor less than the inspiration of the Apostles and their associates; and although, no doubt, the faithful recognised the Divine authority of the men before they recognised the same in their books, yet for all dogmatic purposes our ideas of that inspiration are now derived from the phenomena of the books themselves.

Not only can no Catholic doctrine be shown

to have come down to us by tradition, which is not also to be found in Holy Scripture; it is quite impossible now to extricate the doctrinal tradition of the Church from the influence of Scripture. No doubt tradition is historically older than Scripture, and the Apostles and other primitive teachers had been steadily teaching their doctrines by word of mouth long before they wrote them down. But when once the doctrine was written down, men turned to the written words, especially when the Apostles were not present in person. As, in the particular case of the history of Christ's life on earth, facts and sayings which were not contained in the recognised Gospels soon ceased to pass from mouth to mouth, so with regard to Christian doctrine in general, the New Testament Scriptures soon came to take possession of the whole field of instruction. They were worked up into the living tradition (which, of course, was entirely in harmony with them), until any elements of doctrinal teaching which had begun to be propagated independently of Scripture came to be merged in the new stream of a tradition of which the Scripture was, historically speaking, the source. So much was this the case, that the New Testament Scripture itself bears witness, in some places, to a doctrinal tradition which, because it was not explicitly contained in the written Word, has become extinct. I mention as an instance the detailed teaching which St. Paul gave orally with regard to the Man of Sin, and to the power which restrained his manifestation.[1] There you have a genuine Apostolic doctrine, alive and at work, at Thessalonica and doubtless elsewhere too, which has long ago disappeared from the current teaching of the Church, and has disappeared because of the very fact that it was so well understood at the time as not to need more than an allusive reference from the Apostle's pen, which reference remains now as a crux and an enigma. You cannot say now of any the most simple piece of true Catholic teaching, that it has not come to us out of the Bible.

It was, in the main, to such a tradition as this, into which Scripture had been worked until the

[1] 2 Thess. ii. 6.

two were indistinguishable, that the Fathers appealed when they turned to tradition as against the heretical novelties which sought admission into the Church. When Irenæus, for instance, persuaded men to listen to the voice of the Church, and not to sects who were armed with detached passages of Scripture, because in the Church was preserved the original doctrine of Christianity, he included a reference to the written documents, as well as to the oral preaching which explained them. Even Vincent of Lerins, who appears to speak half-contemptuously about the oracular ambiguity of Scripture as a guide in doctrine, yet shows plainly that the orthodox teaching for which he contends is really taken from Scripture when at last he formulates his charge against the unhappy Origen, whose praises he has been heaping up so rhetorically. "This great and wonderful Origen, presumptuously abusing the grace of God, indulging his own fancy and trusting his own judgment, despising the ancient simplicity of the Christian religion, and pretending to know more than all others put together, scorning

Church traditions and the instructions of the men of old, interpreted" (this is the great crime) "certain passages of the Scriptures in a novel manner."[1] The true tradition of the Church, so Vincent implies, centred in a safe and venerable mode of interpreting the Bible.

We cannot, therefore, treat the tradition of the Church, when contrasted with Scripture, as a co-ordinate source of Christian doctrine, at whatever point in its history we might endeavour to fix that tradition. It is not from the age of the Reformers and the Tridentine theologians; it is not from the age of the Schoolmen, with all their wide outlook, and with all their masterly precision; it is not even from the age of the Fathers, of Athanasius and Augustine,—that we are chiefly to take our doctrine.

The current teaching of the Church, in any age, and in any branch of the Church, needs always to be brought to the test of Scripture. If this test is not vigorously and heedfully applied, the Church is apt to become like the traveller upon a boundless plain without a

[1] Vinc. *Common.* § xvii. (al. 45).

landmark, sure that he is moving in a straight line steadily onwards, who finds at nightfall that he has been marching all day in a curve which has taken him far from the place which he thought to reach. The Fathers, who called upon men to turn from scriptural disquisitions to the living testimony of the Church, had not our length of experience. A test which was useful enough in their time is not so certain to act rightly now. In any Church, at any given period, there are elements of Catholic teaching which are left much out of sight. The age has favourite topics; others are not such favourites. They are, perhaps, not designedly set aside, but they find little active exposition. If it were not for the Scriptures, they would gradually be forgotten or discarded. Now, it is not enough for a healthy Church that the Scriptures should be kept somewhere in the background, as a standard that may be referred to in case of need. Unless they are actually and conscientiously applied, the current teaching wanders further and further away from primitive and Catholic Christianity, and becomes more and more one-sided and abnormal. And if the actual teaching of the day is consciously and on principle set up as of equal value and obligation with the written Word, then the error is made irremediable and hopeless. The Bible must be the informing power in the living teaching of the Church, if that living teaching is to be trustworthy.

It must, of course, never be forgotten that the Bible is a Church book, written by Churchmen for Churchmen, under the inspiration of the same Spirit who is still leading the Church, so far as it is willing to be led, into all truth and in all truth. There are passages of the New Testament which, if isolated from the rest, and read by one who did not know the great principles of the Apostolic doctrine, might easily be thought to mean something far from what is intended. Clever and ingenious persons, approaching the Bible from outside, so to speak, as if it were a newly discovered book, about which there is nothing known, and selecting portions from it after an arbitrary fashion, can make systems out of it that are entirely unlike that which has been received in the Church. This was the way in which, with regard to Church polity, Calvin and the Presbyterians went to work in the sixteenth century. A sound, historical method of study will always pay the utmost deference to what is found to have been the general opinion of Christians of past ages with regard to their faith, and with regard to those books in which their faith is taught; and will only with reluctance and diffidence, if ever, depart from an account which has been generally received. It is to be presumed that the society out of whose bosom the New Testament sprang, and which has all along cherished it as expressing perfectly her own views of God and man, will be the best judge of the construction to be placed upon its utterances.

But this reasonable axiom by no means excludes the necessity of fresh investigations into the meaning of Scripture. In the first place, there are large tracts of the New Testament which have never received any authoritative interpretation, and which abundantly repay study; and, in the second place, even in some instances where it may be said that there is something like an authoritative interpretation, the authority is mainly concerned to assert a general principle of belief which must not be contravened, rather than to assert that the belief is expressed in the text in question. It may be readily conceded that the Church is, in a general sense, the interpreter of Scripture, without holding that a long-current interpretation of a particular passage is critically correct. A position like that of many of the so-called Jansenists is not an illogical one, when they were willing to condemn the propositions laid before them, but refused to acknowledge that those propositions were contained in the writings of Jansen or of Quesnel. The Church is the judge of doctrine; it might not be so safe for her always to claim the right to be the judge of fact.

Whether, however, the Church has this right in the abstract, or not, it is certainly her wisdom to welcome the freest inquiry on the part of her children—and, indeed, of others also—into the meaning of those Scriptures which she recognises as containing the great legacy of her first and most authoritative teachers. There is something—may I say it without offence?—that looks half faithless in the way in which Tertullian and Vincent, but still more the modern writers who quote them with approval, decline the conduct of controversy with heretics over Scripture, as if the Scripture might be made to tell for heresy as easily as against it. It looks as if they thought that Scripture was not only difficult and obscure, but also really dubious. If "Novatian explains it in one way, Sabellius another, Donatus a third, and Arius a fourth,"[1] that is no reason why the inquiry should be surrendered, and the contest fought out upon other fields. The Bible does not *really* mean what first one heretic and then another chooses to make it mean. The sacred writers of the several books were men of sense, who knew what they were saying, although, no doubt, with regard to the Old Testament, the "Spirit of Christ which was in them"[2] caused them

---

[1] Vinc. *Common.* § ii. (al. 5); cp. Tert. *de Præscript.* § 19.
[2] 1 Pet. i. 11.

to utter or write words which were beyond their own full understanding. If not always as perspicuous as impatience might wish, they intended their words to convey one sense, and not another. There is a positively correct interpretation, if it can only be found. Because of the infirmity of all human language, even upon inspired lips, the letter of the text may be patient of more than one meaning; but there is a true and a false way with it. Novatian and Arius cannot really compel it to be their partisan; nor for that matter can the "Catholic sense" either. But the Catholic sense does not need to resort to violence or fraud over the language of the Bible. If the Bible is really what we believe it to be, we can rest secure. The more plainly and simply we can go to work to lay bare the very true signification of the words, the more sure we may be of carrying the argument.

It is, then, unless I am grievously wrong, the best mode of teaching the doctrine of Christ and of His Church, to examine with the most entire candour, and with every aid that criticism can call in, the language of the New Testament. We might hardly have thought that it would be necessary, at this time of day, to fight again the battle which Erasmus began when he published the Notes of Laurentius Valla, and brought down upon himself the fury, as he expected, of those who were the professional theologians of the age. "Intolerable presumption," they will say, "that a mere grammarian, after plaguing all the Schools, should allow his saucy pen to attack even the sacred Books." "I do not think," replies Erasmus, "that even Theology, the queen of all sciences, will disdain the helping hands and dutiful service of her handmaid Grammar—not, perhaps, so distinguished an accomplishment as some, but certainly as necessary as any."[1] It was strange, however, in 1895, to read the apology with which the classical Professor Blass of Halle thought it proper to preface his edition of the Acts of the Apostles, vindicating the rights of the philologist as against a race of professional theologians very different from those confronted by my great Dutch

[1] Ep. ciii. (p. 98 C, E. ed. 1706).

predecessor, but found at length to be no less oppressive to the lay mind of Germany. "The theologians," Blass supposes some one to say to him warningly, "will hardly be content that you have invaded their own province, and all the less because they will think that you despise them, and have no respect for the things on which they specially pride themselves." And, indeed, this brilliant scholar owns that he is inclined to think—and apparently his no less brilliant admirer in our own island, Professor Ramsay, agrees with him—that the great mass of modern scientific German theology is only like a morass on which nothing can be built, and that wherever, as in the Acts of the Apostles, the scientific theologians found firm ground, they have industriously covered it up with mud to look like a morass, in order to have the pleasure of again building upon morasses. This judgment is the judgment of Professor Blass; I do not wish to make it my own.

The help of the linguist cannot, indeed, be too warmly welcomed in the exegesis of the New Testament, and all the more if, in addition to a thorough knowledge of classical Greek, he possesses that historical sense of movement and change in the value of words, which Blass himself so markedly shows. There are, it may be admitted, wide differences in this respect between various New Testament writers; and it would not be safe to apply to a great part of the Acts, or to the Epistle to the Hebrews, a grammatical or philological canon which is required for an exact study of the Gospels, or even of St. Paul. But taking the New Testament Greek as a whole, it seems to me undeniable that, for instance, the indeterminate character of Hebrew tenses, whether directly or through the medium of the LXX., has affected aorists and perfects so that they cannot always be counted upon to mean the same as they would in Thucydides or Plato. With the subsequent history of the conjunction ἵνα in view, it seems to me misleading to insist that everywhere in the New Testament it is to have a final meaning. Again, metaphors that were once fresh and vigorous have become worn-out. An ἐκβάλλειν has ceased to express, in every instance, forcible ejection. An ὑπωπιάζειν no longer means, as we hear affirmed in sermons, to "beat black and blue," though it once had done so. A τραχηλίζειν, which appears to offer so vivid and picturesque a metaphor, disappoints us to the extent of being scarcely able to hazard a guess as to what it originally meant. A κενοῖν, upon which so much has sometimes been made to turn, does not exactly mean "to empty," but has passed through various shades of meaning, such as "to exhaust" (in the natural sense), until it comes to mean something like "to reduce the force, or significance, or reputation of a thing." Instances like these teach us to use caution in the interpretation of the New Testament language. But they by no means teach us, as I have frequently heard it suggested, though never, I think, by Cambridge men, that New Testament Greek cannot be trusted, and that you can drive grammatical accuracy too far. Quite the contrary; they teach that we must seek after a special refinement of accuracy, which may enable us to determine what point in its history a word or a construction has reached, so as to define with perfect precision what it denoted for its writer.

Here in England, and especially at Cambridge, we have long been accustomed to that combination which Professor Blass desires to see, of first-rate linguistic scholars, who are at the same time scientific theologians. The benefit which they have conferred upon Dogmatic Theology by their exegetical work is beyond calculation. What might we not have possessed, if only the series of great Cambridge editions had not come to what seems an untimely end? Alas! we have not been permitted to see a single book of the New Testament edited by the hand of Dr. Hort. How the specimens of exegesis scattered up and down in those little posthumous volumes of his make us long for something more connected in the same line! Meanwhile, Dr. Joseph Mayor has done much to console us for not having one of the works which (as his graceful dedication says) we were desiring, by the extraordinary erudition of his *St. James*. The late Dr. Evans, in his unique manner, gave us some years ago, a Commentary upon the First Epistle to the Corinthians, and Dr. Gifford a Commentary upon the Epistle to the Romans, not undeserving of a place among the great Cambridge Commentaries. The supremacy of the latter among English works on its own subject is now more than threatened by Oxford hands, in the Commentary of my revered schoolfellow who holds the Lady Margaret Professorship there, Dr. Sanday, in collaboration with a younger scholar. But there are sad gaps yet to be filled up. "Sound criticism and explanation of the New Testament records," says Mr. Page of the Charterhouse, in his new schoolbook on the Acts, "must be the basis of Christian theology, but English scholars seem to shrink from the work, so that, for example, there is at the present time no English Commentary on the Synoptic Gospels which is approximately first-rate." There is still plenty of exegetical work to do.

To the ranks of those who are engaged in this work, so far as oral instruction is concerned, I humbly hope for the future to be joined;

and if, in doing so, I aim especially at eliciting the doctrinal conceptions of the great first master-builders of Christian theology, I do not wish it to be thought that I intend to treat their writings as a mere antiquarian storehouse or quarry for criticism. Any one who comes to the study of the Holy Scriptures must, if he would learn their meaning aright, approach them as a living and thrice-sacred thing. If we kneel hushed at Christ's holy Table, knowing that there is more in the Sacrament there offered to us than even faith can fully perceive, so with not less awe must we deal with these words, some of which are His very own, and the rest words that sprang from the hearts of His chosen witnesses under the pressure of the newly given Spirit of God. It would be better for the student himself that he should suffer a partial misunderstanding of the meaning of the words, while his "spirit burns within" him at being admitted to so sublime a colloquy, than that he should draw the most correct conclusions without recognition of the Divine Voice from which he learned them. But for the Church's sake, for the sake of the souls to whom presumably all attendants at a Divinity Professor's lectures are to minister, both things are earnestly to be sought after—the most delicate and exact appreciation of the meaning of the phrases before us, and the adoring discernment of Him who through them is addressing Himself to us.

BISHOP PADDOCK LECTURES.

LECTURE I.

THE HISTORICAL METHOD OF STUDYING OUR LORD'S LIFE UPON EARTH.

AMIDST the anxieties caused by political disagreement, the Church of God serves as a powerful bond between nation and nation, promoting counsels of charity and peace. Blood, the proverb says, is thicker than water; and for this reason England and America ought to be always friends. But there is something which should be more effectual in the maintenance of good relations between country and country than the closest natural ties of race. It is the common devotion to the one Divine Lord, who became the Son of Man, and the Prince of Peace. An English Churchman could not but feel a peculiar pleasure, and even a kind of pride, in observing how the voice of the truly Catholic Bishop of this great city made itself heard a few weeks ago, at a time of popular excitement on this side of the Atlantic, in accents of masculine good sense and Christian moderation. I hope that in a modest way it may contribute something in the same direction, if a student comes from the quiet courts and precincts of Canterbury and Cambridge to speak to American fellow-students about the Lord Jesus Christ, "both theirs and ours."[1] I would wish sincerely to thank those who have done me the honour of inviting me to give these lectures, and I pray that the work may move us all to a more heartfelt and a more intelligent worship of our Blessed Saviour.

The special question which I am permitted to discuss with you, gentlemen, is one of the greatest practical importance for the Christian life. Whatever makes our Blessed Lord a real, living, intelligible figure to the reader of the Gospels has an effect upon men deeper and more powerful than any system of scientific ethics, however convincing that system may be. If Christ is treated as a being of an altogether

[1] 1 Cor. i. 2.

different nature from our own—a God who only assumed a guise of humanity in order to converse visibly with men, without Himself being affected by the nature which He assumed,—then it is vain for us to turn to Him for sympathy, or even for example. In a career of that kind, a pattern might be set before us of a pure and lofty morality ; but, as the motives and feelings which animate the conduct of such a being are not our motives and feelings, therefore, while we may wonder and perhaps adore, we are not greatly inspired to imitate, and hardly even be drawn to love. If Christ is not a man, His life may be a visible embodiment of the Law, but it is not a Gospel,—or only a Gospel inasmuch, as, in consequence of it, for reasons difficult in that case to apprehend, our sins are forgiven us and eternal life is promised. He Himself remains aloof, unknown, unrevealed.

But, on the other hand, a certain current of modern speculations about the life of Christ on earth threatens to rob those whom it touches of some things which we can ill afford to lose. To insist unguardedly upon the appearances of limitation which occur from time to time in the evangelical records, is to imperil our confidence in Christ as a teacher of Divine truth. The mischief lies not always in what such interpreters actually say, but rather in what their teaching seems to imply. If it is suggested that our Lord occasionally, because He knew no better, used arguments which were convincing to those who heard Him, but which rightly fail to convince us, it becomes hard to know why we should be invited to place absolute trust in the accuracy of His revelation as a whole. Supposing that in His condescension to our human conditions He made Himself liable to mistake, can we be sure that He was never mistaken? If He made one assertion without adequate thought or acquaintance with the subject, how can we feel certain that He did not make more such assertions? Clearly it is necessary to look carefully at what the Gospel records convey to us in regard to this matter. May we hope to find that they give us room to believe in an Incarnation which made the Son of God, on the one hand, a true Man like ourselves—only still more truly man,—and, on the other hand, a man capable of bringing to us, by word as well as by deed, a full and unimpeachable manifestation of God?

This question presses upon us at the present day in a manner in which it did not press upon former ages. The ancient Fathers of the Church were little concerned, as a rule, with matters of historical criticism. The debt which we owe to them is not that of having thoroughly sifted questions of this kind. No one can exaggerate the importance of their testimony to the tradition which they had inherited of a Christ who was perfect God and perfect man. Vigilantly and consistently they rejected and refuted every explanation of the Lord's person which infringed this twofold belief—down to the Monotheletism which merged His human faculty of will in the Divine, and to the Adoptianism which made Him in His human nature only gradually to partake of that nearness to the Father which was the property of His person before the Incarnation. Through evil report and good report, like Athanasius, they defended what they justly considered to be a trust committed to them; and, through their labours, it has come down to us unimpaired. We may, indeed, with the utmost profit verify and test their teaching on the Incarnation of Christ, but we can never affect to be independent of it. The definitions of Nicæa and Chalcedon are binding upon us, not only because we have consented to be bound by them under peril of ejection from the Church, but also because the more we work upon the materials at our command, the more abundantly clear it becomes that no theory of the Person of our Redeemer answers to the facts except the theory of the Fathers—two whole and perfect natures coexisting and united in the single and indivisible person of the Son of God made flesh.

This the Fathers did for us. They saved their spiritual descendants from going off into fruitless investigations on the right hand and on the left, and gave them a clear and mighty formula by which to express the cardinal fact of history. But there was much which the Fathers could not do. Each age has its own problems and its own favourite lines of thought. The faith of Christ is too large to have been at all points apprehended by the saints of any age, except by the first inspired teachers. The main object of the Fathers was to set forth the perfect Godhead of Christ: it is hardly too much to say that they were less consciously interested in His manhood. When, indeed, His manhood was directly assailed, as by Docetists, and Manichees, and Apollinarians, the Catholic champions were ready for the defence; but it was upon the other side of the great mystery that they habitually dwelt. How, in the actual experience of that sacred Life, the two natures were accommodated to each other, was not a subject upon which they felt greatly moved to meditate. If occasionally a teacher of unusual vigour and independence, like Hilary of Poitiers, or Cyril of Alexandria, concerns himself with it, we find how great was the practical danger of sacrificing the one half or the other of the great truth,—of surrendering the persistence of the "form of God" when the Lord became man, as sometimes (so far as words go) Hilary does,[1] or of making the manhood practically little more than an appearance, as Hilary more often and Cyril habitually does. It cannot, I think, be doubted that, for one reason and another, the prevailing tone of Christian thought at length tended towards the latter type; and through much of the mediæval theology, which has left its mark deeply imprinted upon the Roman theology of to-day, is observable a minimising tone with regard to our Lord's condescension in becoming man, and a reluctance to admit the entire force of the language of Scripture which makes a solemn reality of His human conditions of life.

Modern studies, often contemptuously impatient of the older teaching, have gone into a different region altogether. Not to speak now of the speculations of the earlier Lutheran divines, like Thomasius, which were primarily theological, and not historical, since the days of Schleiermacher and of Baur the historical spirit has been engaged in endeavouring to

[1] For example, *de Trin.* viii. 45, Exinanivit se ex Dei forma, id est, ex eo quod æqualis Deo erat.

reconstruct the Gospel narrative, with the desire of finding out what it was that actually took place when Jesus sojourned among men. The same critical examination to which, in secular matters, Niebuhr accustomed his contemporaries, has been unsparingly applied to the four Evangelists, and to the New Testament in general. All possible material has been brought together to present to us such a picture of the background of our Saviour's career as is to be found, to name only the crowning instance, in the great work of Schürer. Lives of Christ, from those of Strauss and Renan, to those of Farrar, Geikie, and Edersheim, have endeavoured to familiarise us not only with the scenes amidst which He lived, and the archæology of the period, but also with our Lord's own thoughts and feelings and aims. "Studies in the Gospels"—Trench's, Godet's, Fairbairn's, and many more—seek to throw light upon particular episodes; while books like *Ecce Homo* and *Pastor Pastorum* have taught us, with deep insight and practical sympathy, to watch our Blessed Lord moving before us in the Gospels, as we might watch any other figure, to see for ourselves what He is making for, in general and in detail. Art has followed in the same direction, until M. Tissot has depicted for us a whole Life of Christ, amidst the very scenery of Palestine, and in all the realism of Oriental customs and costumes.

It is, I do not doubt, a wholesome thing for Christian men to be thus brought back to the Christ of history, and to exchange a somewhat distant and intangible conception, such as the reverence of the Church has often held forth, for the sympathetic Jesus in flesh and blood who was presented to the eyes and to the hands of the first disciples. In preaching Christ, we need to return to that which is simple, moving, life-like. Only we must beware that in coming back to the Gospels, we come back without losing or forgetting what we have learned from the Apostolic Epistles and from the Fathers. It would be a grievous mistake if we hoped to learn better the lesson of the Gospels by beginning, as the first disciples did, with everything yet to find out. The mistake is very frequently made. It is assumed by German writers of the stamp of Beyschlag, for example, not to mention still less orthodox names, that the Pauline theology, and of course still more the Johannine, is a speculative addition to the primitive Gospel, —the Gospel which is to be found in its purest form only in St. Mark and certain sections of St. Matthew. According to such teaching we must discard all the later notions of the person of Christ before we can scientifically consider the narrative of His career; and along with the Pauline notions of His person we must discard also those accretions of a mythical kind which, it is supposed, have gathered around the original narrative, such as the stories of Christ's birth and infancy, and of His appearances after the resurrection.

Against this method of reading history we must, in the interests of history as well as of faith, protest. It was a satisfaction to me to be told, gentlemen of this Seminary, that there is among you even a kind of reaction against some of the most modern modes of regarding the life of Christ. Perhaps it is one of the dangers of a comparatively new country like this—in England we consider it to be one of the dangers of Germany—to strive, whether consciously or not, after something novel and advanced, a theory or an analysis that shall eclipse in its brilliant audacity that which attracted observation last year, a desperate anxiety not to be behind the times. I am thankful that you have no such ambitions. A healthy deference to what scholars and devout men have said before us is no bad sign in any Christian community—perhaps least of all in this. If we wish, for some purposes, to study the Gospels afresh, we must do so with all the advantage of the great Creeds for our clue. Instead of beginning, as the first disciples did, with a general disposition indeed to believe in Christ—because John the Baptist had predisposed them to believe,—but not knowing and scarcely guessing what that belief might lead them to, we begin with the results of their completed discipleship. For us, St. John's is the true model of a Gospel, which starts with telling us briefly and solemnly what He is, and then traces the steps by which He came to be recognised as such. We know Him at the outset to be very God of very God; and we desire reverently to observe how this Divine Person acted and felt in the new conditions into which He vouchsafed to come.

In order that any inquiry may be made in a scientific manner, it is necessary, in the first instance, to make sure of the facts. To frame a theory first, and then support it by such facts as seem capable of being forced into the service, while ignoring all facts of an opposite character, is never likely to lead to a sound result. Men may indeed frame tentative hypotheses, to see how they will work; but such must be modestly put forward, and their authors must be ready to abandon them, or modify them, when a larger observation of the facts demands it. This holds true with regard to the life of our Blessed Lord, as much as it does with regard to any other scientific inquiry. It is not my purpose in these lectures to maintain a theory, though very likely something of a theory may naturally result from the study before us. Rather I wish to make a somewhat comprehensive survey of the phenomena of the case, in order that we may judge how far those phenomena are in agreement with any of the particular theories that have held the field in ancient times or in modern. In order to see, as far as it may be given us to see, how the two natures met in the actual experience of our Lord, we shall do well not to insist upon preconceived notions of how they must have met, but rather to look carefully at what He said about Himself, and what others remarked in Him.

In this connexion I need make no apology for using the Gospels with absolute confidence. There are many interesting questions as yet unanswered with regard to the composition of the Gospels—especially of the first three. The problem of the Fourth Gospel (which is, of course, for theological purposes, the most important) is a simpler problem; and I believe it to have been in the main solved. Although critics like Jülicher still hold back from acknowledging that Gospel to be the work of the Apostle John, I cannot but think that such scepticism (though in Jülicher's case of a moderate and fairly reverent kind) is belated and retrogressive.[1] Not only is the external testimony to this Gospel of a singularly clear and cogent kind,—not only are its delineations of character, and of parties among the Jews, and so on, entirely beyond the range of a composer of the second century, —but from the time of Renan's *Vie de Jésus* onwards, men not swayed by ecclesiastical prepossessions have seen that it contains historical information of the highest value, which in some cases corrects a false impression which might have been left upon us by the Synoptic Gospels, and in other cases supplements them in a way which makes their account for the first time intelligible. How far the discourses of our Lord recorded in it have been abridged, systematized, altered in phraseology by long meditation in the mind of the Evangelist, may be matter for speculation or investigation; but I do not think it can be doubted that the twentieth

---

[1] Perhaps we are not so much alarmed as some might be at the form of "academic terrorism" which uses the threat—they are Jülicher's own words—that, if the Apostle John wrote this Gospel, then 2 Peter might be the work of Simon Peter (*Einleit. in. d. N.T.*, p. 255).

century will pay more deference to the Gospel of St. John than the nineteenth has done, and that as the tendency of free criticism has been to accept more and more of the Pauline Epistles as genuine, so the tendency will be to see in the Fourth Gospel that which it claims for itself, to be the work of the disciple whom Jesus loved.

The inter-relation of the three Synoptists is more difficult to determine, and perhaps the questions concerning it will never be set at rest. None of the theories which have been propounded are free from difficulty; and we still await the discoverer of the master scheme. But even those who think that they discern legendary elements in St. Matthew and St. Luke, or even in the present form of St. Mark, are ready nowadays for the most part to confess the sobriety and good faith of the narrators and the inherent likelihood of the portrait of Jesus which in the main they draw. For us who belong to the Catholic Church it is a matter of comparative indifference who wrote our Gospels, and how they came to write them.

We accept the four Gospels as the early Church accepted them, as conveying to us the Holy Spirit's manifold delineation of the life and character of our Redeemer. It may be true that none of the four was, in the first instance, written as a mere history; they are works of edification, and interpretations of the history:[1] but for our purpose they are all the more valuable for that. They show us the views of Christ entertained by, to say the least of it, the highest, soundest, most representative teachers in the Church of the first century, as distinguished from the fantastic, inconsistent, and unsatisfying conceptions of the Gospel-makers of the century after. If Jesus Christ is a historical character at all, this is what He was; and He must have been such as they describe, in order to produce the effect upon His followers which we know that He produced.

And not only do we feel a just confidence in the general portraiture of Christ which the Gospels contain; we believe that even in the detailed expressions the superintendence of

[1] Jülicher *Einl.* p. 184; cp. p. 230.

the Holy Spirit has been at work. Taking
Christ for our guide, we are bound to acknowledge that even in the Old Testament nothing
is accidental and insignificant. "The Scripture
cannot be broken," or "undone."[1] So He said
one day, with regard to what might have
seemed to us but a casual or conventional
phrase in one of the Psalms. It would have
been easy, and perhaps not irreverent, to have
thought that the words, "I said, Ye are gods,"
were an ordinary instance of Eastern hyperbole
—that "gods" does not really contain the tremendous meaning which has grown into the
word. But such explanations did not satisfy our
Lord. He saw in the use of that language,
whatever may have been the process by which
it came to be so used, a witness in the Jewish
"law" that Godhead is not so far off, so incommunicable, as they thought; and He said that
those who would reduce the expression to a
poetical exaggeration were breaking up or undoing the Scripture. If this be so, no Christian
can doubt that every sentence, and every turn of

[1] St. John x. 35: οὐ δύναται λυθῆναι.

a sentence, in the New Testament has been at least as much the object of the inspiring Spirit's care. There, as elsewhere, it may not have been always His design to secure a literal, a pedantic, exactitude of historical statement. Who cares, for instance, whether there were two demoniacs healed at Gadara, or one; two blind men at the gate of Jericho, or one? So long as we may be certain that the Evangelists in such matters were honest and truthful, sought the best information, and never fabricated or embellished the events which they narrate, it is enough for us. The minutiæ of the narrative in such matters go for little. But it is otherwise with phrases which have a bearing upon the very person and character of the Lord Himself. Here the Evangelists utter the mind of the Church of their own illuminated time. Any thing that was out of keeping with that conception of Christ which the Apostles had inculcated upon the Church, would have jarred upon the sensibilities of the assemblies of the faithful, in which the Gospels were read aloud. The more we admit that the works of the

Evangelists are primarily works of edification rather than of history, the more we feel that we can rely upon their representations of Christ's person. And as the tendency in the Church was to distrust more and more any language which might be thought derogatory to Christ's Divine power and knowledge, we may with the greater attentiveness observe those sayings which particularly emphasize the human nature and the voluntary humiliation of the Son of God. Such sayings are a sign of an early date, and of the historical, as opposed to the romantic, character.

And certainly, the more we read them, the more we feel that the Gospels—St. John's as much as any—contain the history of a Man indeed. We do not often, it is true, use that term in speaking of our Saviour, because it requires to be guarded. To say that He was "a Man" seems for the moment to imply that He was a man and nothing more; and we should utterly misunderstand the Gospels if we saw in them the story of one who was only a man. And, besides this, when Christ is called "a Man," it sounds as if He were considered only an incidental specimen of the race, like one of ourselves, and not, as He is in fact, the universal Man, in whom the whole of human nature is gathered up—the Representative and Head of the entire species. Nevertheless, this language is used of Him in the New Testament, and there is a certain loss in shrinking from applying it to Him. It is not only the hostile, or casual, or uninstructed onlookers in the Gospels who call Him so, as they naturally would,—"We know that this man is a sinner," "Come, see a man that told me all things that ever I did." Our Lord condescends to call Himself so. "Ye seek to kill Me, a Man ($ἄνθρωπον$) that hath told you the truth."[1] St. Paul calls Him so. "There is one Mediator between God and men, the Man ($ἄνθρωπος$) Christ Jesus."[2] And sometimes a still more significant word in the original is used. The word $ἀνήρ$ differs from $ἄνθρωπος$, not only in distinguishing the sex—man as opposed to woman; it brings out the fulness of personal dignity. If a company

---

[1] St. John viii. 40.   [2] 1 Tim. ii. 5.

of men is addressed by the title of ἄνθρωποι, they are appealed to on the strength of their common nature; if they are addressed as ἄνδρες, they are appealed to on the strength of their distinct individuality. And this is the bold word which is several times employed in the New Testament in speaking of our Lord. It is placed by the Evangelist St. John in the mouth of the Baptist: "This is He of whom I said, After me cometh a Man (ἀνήρ) who hath been preferred before me, because He was before me;"[1] and by St. Luke in that of Cleopas on the evening after the Resurrection: ἐγένετο ἀνὴρ προφήτης [2]—a respectful turn of phrase, which cannot be rendered in English. St. Peter, on the day of Pentecost, so describes our Lord: "Jesus of Nazareth, a Man (ἄνδρα) displayed unto you by God;"[3] and St. Paul at Athens, speaking of that which is now present and is yet to come, still ascribes to our Lord that fulness—His own, and not another's—of personal human life, when he says that God intends "to judge the world in righteousness

---

[1] St. John i. 30.   [2] St. Luke xxiv. 19.   [3] Acts ii. 22.

(ἐν ἀνδρὶ ᾧ ὥρισεν) in a Man whom He marked out."[1]

We may, then, with good reason, expect to see a truly human life lived out before us in the scenes which the Gospels record. And wonderful it is that the sacred historians, writing at a time when the thought of believers had undergone so great a change with regard to Christ,—when by the Holy Spirit they knew Him no longer after the flesh,—should have been able so simply to relate the events which took place before that change of thought came. Knowing Him to be indeed, and to have been throughout, very God of very God, they have yet set down for us, in a manner which nothing short of inspiration could have accomplished, truthfully and without exaggeration, the life as it was actually lived, so that in the words of Erasmus, which have of late years been brought to the notice of so many in the beginning of Westcott's and Hort's Greek Testament, "They reproduce the living image of that sacred mind, and bring before us Christ Himself, speaking, healing, dying, rising again,

[1] Acts xvii. 31.

present in every aspect, in such a way that we should less truly see Him, if we were able to fix upon Him our very eyes."

It is not strange that the four Gospels, which thus set Him before us, have received, in the Catholic Church, an honour beyond even those inspired Epistles or those inspired Prophecies which interpreted, before or after, the person and the work of Christ. They were enthroned at the great Councils of the early Church, that Christ in them might, as it were, speak for Himself. The ancient ritual of the Church surrounded the reading of them with expressive symbolism. None below the order of Deacons might read them aloud to the assembly. Others might read the Epistle; and the people might sit at their ease to listen to it. But it was otherwise with the Holy Gospel. With solemn procession and special benedictions, with lighted tapers and incense, and with acclamations, while all sprang to their feet, and the priest turned round from his station at the altar, the sacred words were read aloud which Christ either spoke Himself, or which described some mighty action of His. It is, in truth, a Real Presence of Christ which comes among us at such a time. The holy Sacrament of His Body and Blood does not more surely bring Him to us than this, His blessed Word. In the Gospels we may reverently study Him for ourselves, and mark His very gestures and the emotions of His heart. No less than the first disciples themselves, though with fuller knowledge than they at the time possessed, we may become spectators of each solemn event ; and questioning Him, as they did, where we do not understand, we may, if we will, attain by His grace to a knowledge of Him and His ways which is not transmitted and remote, but direct and immediate.

LECTURE II.

THE DEVELOPMENT OF OUR LORD'S MORAL CHARACTER AS MAN.

ASSUMING that we may rely with entire confidence upon the Gospels, and upon the inspired comments of the New Testament writers, for guidance in the accomplishment of our task, we proceed to examine with all reverence what is disclosed to us of the conditions under which our Blessed Lord lived His life as a true Man upon earth. We begin with the development of His ethical character. Character is the moral configuration of the soul, which results from the grouping and blending of the various kinds of moral habits; which habits are themselves the product of repeated acts of moral choice, made amidst the changing circumstances of life and in accordance with, or in defiance of, the natural bent of temperament.

It must be said at the outset, that both the record of the facts, and our knowledge of what Christ is, make plain the inference that He came into our world without that vitiation of His first human movements which we call by the name of original sin. He alone was conceived without sin, because, as St. Bernard says, He alone was holy before His conception.[1] It is not possible that He should have been willing to attach to Himself a nature which was actually corrupt, as some have dreamed.

Indeed, I do not see how, with any clearness of mind, we can think of sin, or of holiness either, as inherent in a nature, distinguished from the personalities who possess that nature. Those who, following Edward Irving, imagine our Lord to have assumed humanity in a fallen and depraved condition, are really, without knowing it, reaffirming, in another form, the Manichæan doctrine that matter is itself

[1] Bern. *Ep.* clxxiv.

evil.[1] They attach moral attributes, not to the movements of the personal will, but to the stuff upon which and through which the will has to work. This is a radically false and unchristian conception of ethical good and evil. Sin does not reside in flesh, as flesh, or in nature, as nature, but in the choice made by personal wills, whether they be the wills of creatures in fleshly nature, or the wills of creatures in other natures. By the mysterious law which links together the fortunes of all the free-willed beings who come of the stock of Adam and are but men, the very earliest stirrings of personal human life are not free from moral evil; but the evil lies in the way in which those personalities themselves act, and not in the accidental circumstances into which they are plunged. If men were not themselves sinners, but only spirits unwillingly involved in bad conditions, then they would deserve nothing but pity, and not blame. The guilt of sin lies in the man himself, not in his nature apart from

[1] See Mill's remarks, in his *Five Sermons on the Temptation*, pp. 35, 152, 153 (ed. 1844).

him. And if sin could be supposed to lie in a nature, or in certain conditions of a nature, apart from the personal will of those who belong to that nature, then for any one willingly to enter into that nature so conditioned must needs be a sinful act, whatever might be the ultimate purpose of the act. Incarnation into sinful flesh would be, not a condescension, but a fall. The Son of God could not begin His work of redemption by an act of sin. He could only take into conjunction with His holy person such elements and in such conditions as were capable of the conjunction, and could serve for the manifestation of a holy will. Christ never had our primary difficulty of overcoming a hereditary disposition to go wrong. He was as unimpeded in the formation of His moral character as was the first Adam, who was created with all his faculties perfect, and with every impulse wholesome.

To this pure and beautiful new beginning of the human race in Christ the appropriate avenue was His conception by a Virgin Mother. I do not know whether the strife which is still vehemently surging among the German Protestants upon this subject has aroused much attention in America. It cannot, at any rate, cause any division of opinion within our own Catholic communion, which day by day repeats its affirmation that Christ was conceived by the Holy Ghost, and born of the Virgin Mary. If the narratives at the beginning of St. Matthew and St. Luke are legends which sprang up somewhere in the early Church after the days of the Apostles, we cannot but marvel at the incomparable moderation and the delicacy, beyond that of the highest of poets, which existed among those first Christians, to invent, and to leave so chastely unadorned, the story of the Manger, and the Shepherds, and the Wise Men, and the Presentation, and the Finding in the Temple. It is a strange kind of historical or literary criticism which finds it easier to suppose that these narratives are the creation of fancy than the recollections respectively of St. Joseph and of the Blessed Virgin Mary. Signs are not wanting that already a more critical spirit than that which is so often vaunted is bringing men round, even in Germany, to a more reasonable view. Professor Loofs of Halle, the most respected of the disciples of Professor Harnack, is able, so I am told, to set himself so far free from his master's influence as to say that, in a life where miracles cannot be denied, one miracle more or less makes little difficulty, and that therefore the virgin Conception may be admitted.[1] But such grounds for the admission—so welcome in itself —are most inadequate. They might, perhaps, have sufficed to secure acquiescence for that which is really a legend, the legend of the virgin Birth, as distinguished from the virgin Conception, if it had found its way into the sacred text; but it has not. From a very early period, and with a strange unanimity, Church teachers inculcated the belief that, not only was the Lord conceived without earthly fatherhood, but that at birth He came to the light by a process unknown to ordinary nature, which they supposed to be necessary to the preservation of

---

[1] In his three Sermons on the *Apostolicum*, preached before the University of Halle, Professor Loofs treats the matter as not of "fundamental" importance (p. 21, footnote).

His Mother's virgin estate. It is a good instance of the difference between the miracles of Scripture and the clumsy fancies of men. If Scripture had taught us that our Lord came forth from His mother's womb in the same manner as He came into the Upper Chamber where the doors were shut, we should, I dare say, have bowed to authority; but we should have felt our faith to be tried by the imposition of a miracle which would be not only gratuitous and unimpressive, but also actually misleading, because it would have obscured the difference between the Lord's natural body and His resurrection body. The miracle of His conception, on the other hand, can scarcely be said to be a miracle at all, so completely does it seem to be demanded—though assuredly it was not invented afterwards to meet the demand—by the fact that His birth was not, like ours, the first inception of a new personality, but the advent of an already existent and Divine person upon a new mode of being.

The Incarnate Lord begins, then, without our disadvantage of original sin. But to start in human life with untainted springs of desire and thought, is not the same thing as to have attained the perfection of moral character. Perfection is not, in our changeful existence, a stationary thing. The human being who begins with the perfection of a babe, must go on to the more conscious and voluntary perfection of the grown man; and this can only be attained, so far as we can see, through temptations fully felt and persistently overcome. Christ, therefore, became the subject of temptation.

We might, perhaps, never have imagined that Christ was tempted, if He had not Himself disclosed the fact to His disciples. Probably in their reverent admiration for His even, unwavering career of goodness, they would not have allowed themselves to suppose that it ever cost Him an effort to be good. They would have thought that it came to Him—as we have seen that, in part, it did—by nature, and would have shrunk from thinking of Him as undergoing any hard hand-to-hand conflict with the solicitations of evil. Few parts of the Gospel narrative are so little likely to be the result of the legend-making process as the description of the Temptation of our Saviour after His Baptism. It wears, indeed, a symbolic form, like that of the temptation of our first parents. In no other form could we rightly apprehend the temptations which presented themselves to the mind of God made man. But that the disciples should themselves have invented such a beginning for their Master's public ministry is as impossible as that they should have invented its closing with the Agony in the Garden and the cry of dereliction on the Cross. It must have been to them a moment of shock and of terror when our Lord first confided to them what He had passed through.

But when once told that our Lord was tempted, it is not difficult for us to suppose that He was often, that He was constantly tempted. Such a special crisis, perhaps, never occurred again, but it would be unnatural to suppose that no temptations had ever occurred to Him before, in boyhood and in youth; and we are permitted to know of occasions when they distinctly occurred to Him afterwards. Indeed, the Evangelist significantly says, at the close of his account of the great Temptation, that "the devil departed from Him" only "for a season."[1] Sometimes temptations came to Him through the voice of friends. I do not know what else can account for the sudden severity of tone with which He repels His Mother's appeal the instant before working His first miracle.[2] Nothing else accounts for the terrific severity with which He displayed the character of St. Peter's argument, when once the Apostle undertook to cheer—as he must have thought—the failing spirits of his Master, and to stop Him from taking so gloomy a view of the situation. "Get thee behind Me, Satan," was the reply, identifying the well-meaning but misguided friend with the dreadful agency which made use of him; and then followed the confession which showed how sharp the temptation to our Saviour Himself had been—" For thou art an offence, a cause of stumbling, unto Me."[3] He felt in that hour what martyrs have felt, when fathers and brothers and friends have

[1] St. Luke iv. 13.   [2] St. John ii. 4.   [3] St. Matt. xvi. 23.

offered a means of escape, and urged, "Spare thy youth," or "Spare thy old age," and was not too proud—when it was wholesome for His disciple to be warned—to show how acutely the suggestion had been felt. At other times, and, we may well believe, less dangerously, the temptation came through the lips of enemies, repeating, as they did during the Crucifixion, the very words which expressed once more His temptation in the wilderness, "If Thou be the Son of God, if Thou be the Christ, save Thyself." And that which found distinct utterance at such moments must have been discerned by our Lord's keen perceptions on a thousand unrecorded occasions as well. As He looks back upon the years of His ministry from the Upper Chamber the night before His death, He says to the faithful eleven, "Ye are they which have continued with Me in My temptations,"[1] as if these had been the main feature of His life during the three years and a half of the Apostles' association with Him.

The great unknown interpreter of the life

[1] St. Luke xxii. 28.

of Christ, the writer of the Epistle to the Hebrews, to whom it was given, more than to any other of the inspired writers, to draw out for us the significance of the human nature of our Lord, generalises the typical temptation after our Lord's Baptism by saying that He "was in all points tempted like as we are, without sin."[1] It is a bold generalisation, but not unwarranted—indeed, St. Luke himself made or accepted it, when, at the close of his account of the forty days in the wilderness, he says that the devil only left our Lord, "when he had brought to a conclusion all temptation."[2] However temptations may be sorted and classified, they are all represented there,—temptations of the component parts of man, body, soul, and spirit; temptations through the main foes with which we are confronted, the world, the flesh, and the devil; temptations to sin against God, and self, and the world, through omission of duty, and through doing, in thought, word, and deed,

---

[1] Heb. iv. 15.
[2] St. Luke iv. 13: συντελέσας πάντα πειρασμόν.

what should not be done. "In all points," He was tempted. He had all our faculties, and all our attractions and repulsions. Sweet was sweet to Him, and bitter was bitter. Labour and repose were to Him what they are to us. Nay, His capacities for enjoyment and for pain, in mind and in body, were immeasurably beyond ours; and, in all this vast range, there was no spot where temptation did not assail Him, with a subtlety, a pertinacity, an intensity, of which we have little notion. Some measure of the strength of His temptation in the wilderness may be gathered from the words of St. Matthew and St. Luke, when they tell us that, "when He had fasted forty days and forty nights, He was afterward an hungred;" "when the days were accomplished, He hungered."[1] Read these words in conjunction with St. Mark's brief statement that He was "forty days tempted of the devil,"[2] and the meaning of that "afterwards" will appear. It would seem that under the stress of the temptation He had no leisure during those forty days to

[1] St. Matt. iv. 2; St. Luke iv. 2.   [2] St. Mark i. 13.

pay attention to His bodily wants—even as, upon the Cross, it was only after the horror of His great darkness began to pass away that He gave utterance to His consciousness of thirst. Truly temptation was a fearful reality to our Blessed Saviour.

The language of the Epistle to the Hebrews carries us a step further, when it says that not only was He in all points tempted, but was tempted "like as we are (καθ' ὁμοιότητα)." Temptation did not come to Him in a fashion that made it different from what we know; it was the same. We are not indeed compelled to suppose that temptations presented themselves to Him in the same forms in which they come to us. If they had done so, they would, in many cases, have lost all their tempting power. Sensuality or worldliness in the coarse forms in which they make havoc of the souls of men could never have been anything but an object of hatred and disgust to His pure soul. It was necessary that temptation should come to Him in the most refined and insidious form if there was to be the least ground for supposing that it might succeed. But when it came in an appropriate form, it came to Him as it comes to us. It needed the exercise of vigilance and a sensitive conscience to discern its character; it cost effort, strength of will, pain and hardship to resist. And the fact that He was "without sin," while it freed Him, doubtless, from many of our worst temptations, only added to the acuteness of others. He never knew by experience of His own, what we know too well, the force with which temptation comes to us again on the score of having been yielded to before, nor the difficulty of going back from a position once wrongly taken up. But on the other hand, our dulled and hardened consciences can ill imagine the poignancy of the torture which it must have been to one who was wholly right and good, to be besieged and assaulted with every manner of solicitation to fall away from His lofty standard of duty. We can see that, being what He was, it was inconceivable that He should really fall; but none the less —perhaps we should say, all the more—He was permitted to experience to the full all the hardship of doing right.

This brings us to the question, which is of profound interest for us,—how "the Man Christ Jesus" held His ground, and not only remained sinless amidst temptation, but also formed by the conflict that holiness of human character which makes Him the pattern for all other men to follow. Did He bear down the temptation by summoning up the forces of His own Divine nature,—that Godhead which "cannot —be tempted of evil,"[1]—or did He meet it as a creature may, by loyal dependence upon God His Father? I dare say that many of us in childhood supposed that when our Lord replied to the temptation to cast Himself from the pinnacle in the words, "Thou shalt not tempt the Lord thy God," He was rebuking Satan for his wickedness in tempting *Him*, and asserting His Divine superiority to the temptation. In point of fact, the words seem to indicate clearly the opposite thought,—that He had taken upon Himself the estate of a subject and a servant,

[1] St. James i. 13.

and was bound to do nothing, and would do nothing, that might "tempt the Lord." The Lord was His God. To cast Himself down from the pinnacle would have been to claim the aid of His God for an action not dictated by Him; and so would have provoked the Lord His God to withdraw that aid upon which He relied. In like manner, the replies to the other temptations set plainly before us how entirely our Saviour had thrown Himself into the position of human dependence. "Man shall not live by bread alone," and Christ was man. He lived, as other men may and ought to live, by "every word that proceedeth out of the mouth of God." He would not pay an act of homage to the Tempter, because He was under the law for man, and that law laid it upon Him to worship the Lord His God, and to serve no other instead of Him, or in conjunction with Him. This language is not like that of one who draws upon forces within Himself, whether human or superhuman, for the conflict with temptation. It is the language of one who occupies a creaturely place, and trusts in the aid of the Creator.

We must see whether this view is borne out by other indications given to us in Holy Scripture.

The rigour of the mediæval theology, which is still held binding by Roman divines, denies that our Blessed Lord, when He was upon earth, was capable of faith. He had, they say, at all times the Beatific Vision; and where vision is, there faith cannot be. I confess that it seems to me a shallow conception of faith, thus absolutely to contrast it with sight, and to think that it comes to an end when sight is vouchsafed. Although St. Paul in one place speaks of faith as opposed to sight,[1] in another place he speaks (and it is surely his habitual view of the matter) of faith as "abiding," even when we shall know as we were known.[2] It is a virtue of the soul which is specially tested by the absence of sight, as of other forms of demonstration; but the virtue does not cease when its trials are over. But even if this were otherwise, the correctness of the mediæval reasoning might be doubted. The Bible does not tell us, in so many words, that our Lord in

[1] 2 Cor. v. 7. [2] 1 Cor. xiii. 13.

His life on earth enjoyed the Beatific Vision, and we are not bound, therefore, either to affirm or to deny it. The Bible does assure us that He lived, in the largest sense, a life of faith. He was, says the Epistle to the Hebrews, "faithful unto Him that made Him (what He was) in all His house,"[1] even as Moses had been. If the predominant thought here is that of fidelity in the discharge of duty, it yet emphasizes a relationship from which faith, in the full acceptation, cannot be excluded. Jesus is again described as "the Captain and Perfecter of faith"—not "of our faith,"[2] as the Old Version wrongly glosses. He first showed what faith really was, and set a complete and faultless example of it, the contemplation of which may animate us to endure trials which have some resemblance to His own. And when the great writer, whose words we have been quoting, would furnish a text of the Old Testament which should fully express the moral and spiritual position adopted by the Eternal Son on coming into

---

[1] Heb. iii. 2.
[2] Heb. xii. 2, Τῆς πίστεως ἀρχηγὸς καὶ τελειωτής.

the world, the text is, "And I will put My trust in Him."[1] He had all the Old Testament to choose from, and it may seem strange that he chose this text; but the force of the passage is unquestionable. The attitude of the typical prophet, or of the theocratic king (for it is not certain whose words they are in the first instance), is that of a trust absolutely fixed once for all upon God; and such was the attitude which Christ would assume. Renouncing all trust in Himself, or in any creaturely aid, or in earthly modes of attaining to success, this was to be His one motto through life, unswerving reliance upon God, whatever God might call upon Him to suffer or to do. The fall of man in the beginning had come about through distrust of God's ordering of things, and the assertion of human independence; and He who came to undo the fall would undo it through the opposite course unflinchingly adhered to,—abnegation of self, and confident dependence upon God.

Thus, when a young man full of religious

[1] Heb. ii. 13, Ἐγὼ ἔσομαι πεποιθὼς ἐπ' αὐτῷ.

ardour came to our Lord, and asked Him, "Good Master, what good thing shall I do that I may attain eternal life?" our Lord replied to him in a manner which must at first have sounded strangely disheartening, "Why callest thou Me good? there is none good but One, that is God."[1] It cannot mean that Christ is refusing in one capacity an epithet which, in another capacity, He would have accepted; as if He had said to the young man, "You think Me to be a good man: I am not that; I am God, and only by virtue of My divine nature am I to be called good." Besides other insurmountable difficulties in such an interpretation, it could have furnished no guidance to one who was earnestly asking for guidance. The inquirer could not have been expected to hit upon such an interpretation of the words. Nor, on the other hand, assuredly, did our Saviour mean to say, "You are mistaken in Me; I am not what you think Me: My life, though possibly better than that of most men, is yet faulty when examined as God examines; I, like the

[1] St. Mark x. 18.

rest of us, am a sinner; for goodness you must look away from Me." Not a single word of Christ elsewhere would support such a view of His meaning here. It is allowed on all hands that penitence and the consciousness of imperfection, which are so characteristic of all the saints, and of the best most, are entirely absent from the life of Christ. When He says, "Why callest thou Me good? there is none good but One, that is God," He is saying what may help His interlocutor to attain that which he desires to attain; and the meaning is surely this—Christ is not only our pattern, as I have said, but our example; and His methods of attaining to moral perfection are our methods. He will not allow the rich young ruler to imagine that His goodness proceeds from within Himself, and that there is some secret by which the young man, too, can be taught to make himself good with a self-made goodness, and worthy of eternal life. Such a notion could only start the man again upon that weary path of Pharisaic self-righteousness which inevitably ends in failure and bitter disappointment. "If you think Me good," He seems to say, " I can assure you that that goodness comes from a source that is higher than Myself, and that source is one from which you also may draw. The only way in which human character can be trained for eternal life is by humble constant waiting, hanging, upon God."

In keeping with this view of our Lord's life as a life of faith is the fact that it was a life of prayer. The prayers were, no doubt, largely on behalf of others, but not in every instance. St. Mark records how, the morning after His first great healing at Capernaum, "rising up early while it was still long before day, He went out into a solitary place, and there prayed,"[1] until Simon and his companions pursued Him to the spot; and how, after the feeding of the Five Thousand, when it was late, He dismissed the disciples and then the multitude, and "went away into the mountain to pray."[2] St. Luke records that it was while He was praying, after His Baptism, that the Holy Ghost descended upon Him;[3] he mentions

[1] St. Mark i. 35.   [2] St. Mark vi. 46.   [3] St. Luke iii. 21.

it as a feature of our Lord's first evangelistic circuit in Galilee, that "He was wont to retire in the solitudes and pray."[1] Before the setting apart of the Twelve, "He went out into the mountain," says St. Luke, "and continued the whole night in prayer to God."[2] "It came to pass," says the same Evangelist, relating the confession at Cæsarea Philippi, "that His disciples were with Him,"—or, according to another reading, "His disciples met with Him"—"as He was praying by Himself."[3] His Transfiguration took place, according to St. Luke, when, "taking with Him Peter and John and James, He went up into the mountain to pray."[4] It was, says St. Luke, "when He was in a certain place praying, that, when He ceased, one of His disciples said unto Him, Lord, teach us to pray."[5] All three Synoptists record the last tremendous prayer in Gethsemane. St. Luke records His marvellous intercession for those who crucified Him. Even St. John, whom many critics accuse of making

---

[1] St. Luke v. 16. [2] St. Luke vi. 12. [3] St. Luke ix. 18.
[4] St. Luke ix. 28. [5] St. Luke xi. 1.

our Lord's life on earth purely Divine, twice gives the words of His address to the Father. The first, though not a prayer, is a direct thanksgiving that a previous prayer had been accepted,—"Father, I thank thee that Thou didst hear Me," and implies a constant habit of prayer,—"I knew that Thou hearest Me always;"[1] the second is His great intercession for the disciples and for their converts.[2] The same Evangelist represents Him as promising to continue His prayers even after His departure from the earth,[3] and, in His first Epistle, speaks of Him as our "Advocate with the Father."[4] St. Matthew, though he speaks of no prayer of Christ's except that in the Garden of Gethsemane, records that most significant saying, "Thinkest thou that I cannot beseech My Father, and He shall this instant send Me more than twelve legions of angels?"[5] and the words in which, addressing God first as "Father," then as "Lord of heaven and earth," our Saviour gives thanks for the failure of His

[1] St. John xi. 41, 42.   [2] St. John xvii.   [3] St. John xiv. 16.
[4] 1 John ii. 1.   [5] St. Matt. xxvi. 53.

work in one direction, and the success given to it in another which seemed less promising,—" I thank Thee that Thou didst hide these things from the wise and prudent, and didst reveal them unto babes;" submitting Himself by a sublime act of faith to the plan so declared: "Even so, Father, for so it seemed good in Thy sight."[1] The thanksgiving is followed by the two utterances, in such strange juxtaposition,—that all things had been delivered to Him by the Father, and that the condition of obtaining the rest which He offered was to learn of Him meekness and lowliness of heart.

The juxtaposition, I say, of these two utterances seems strange; and yet it is the natural outcome of Christ's whole life. He wins by submission. He is exalted through obedience. It is by taking to the uttermost the "form of a servant" that He attains "the name which is above every name." It is indeed significant that the one virtue in His own character to which our Incarnate Lord directs attention is this, of "meekness and lowliness of heart." He

[1] St. Matt. xi. 25 foll.

might with good reason have said, "Learn of Me, for I am pure, am just, am brave, am truthful;" but these virtues, though as fully developed in Him as any, were not the virtues which put His life into the most marked contrast, not only with those of other men, but also with what might have been expected of Him. Self-will, the choosing for ourselves, is the prevailing aspect of our conduct in the world; "we have turned every one to his own way." With Him, the prevailing aspect is that of a cheerful and glad obedience: "I seek not Mine own will, but the will of Him that sent Me."[1]

How difficult that will was to do, every one has endeavoured to discern who has thought at all of the Cross of Christ. His devotion to the will of God was tested by every form of suffering which the craft and malice of the devil or man could bring to bear upon it,— nay, it may be said that God Himself tried His Incarnate Son to the utmost. Little deserving of suffering though He was, He was

[1] St. John v. 30.

early put into that painful school, and He continued in it to the end. And it was indeed to Him a school, in which lesson succeeded to lesson in due order and gradation. Had He died by the sword of Herod at Bethlehem, we dare not say that the sacrifice would have been insufficient for the salvation of the world; but we may safely affirm that the little human Babe could not have accomplished the work of redemption in the same intelligent and active way as He did when He was grown up. It was a gradual process by which He was practised for the final contest. "He wakeneth morning by morning"—so says Christ beforehand, by the prophet,—"He wakeneth Mine ear to hear as the learned."[1] It is, as any Hebrew reader knows, the technical language of the scholar and the master. Even as He bade us to take up our cross daily and follow Him, so He Himself received daily the instruction in suffering which was appropriate for the day. Had the last trials come to Him near the beginning,

[1] Isa. l. 4.

He might not have been able to bear them, but might have died prematurely in making the effort. On Him, as on us, God laid no greater burden than He was able to bear. And so, at last, He "who, though He was the Son, yet learned obedience by the things which He suffered," became "perfect through sufferings"[1] with a perfection which could not be improved by any prolongation. The Cross, following upon the Garden of Gethsemane, was the final lesson by which the human character of our Lord was brought to its absolute and unsurpassable perfection. Obedience, the supreme virtue of the creature, could be carried no higher; and He who was thus made perfect by obeying God, became "the cause of eternal salvation to all those who in turn obey *Him.*"[2]

All the phenomena of Christ's inward experience during His life on earth which are recorded for us, combine to suggest that His moral growth—as He "increased in favour with God,"[3] and with the men of God—was of the

[1] Heb. ii. 10.   [2] Heb. v. 9.   [3] St. Luke ii. 52.

same kind as ours at its best, only so immeasurably better. It is thus that we are invited to reckon upon the completeness of His sympathy with us in all our moral struggles and the difficulties of maintaining a right relalation with the will of God. Had Christ's earthly life been that of a God, to whom His earthly nature was little more than a veil and a semblance, then it might have been possible to say of Him, as the Psalmists said of God, " He knoweth whereof we are made; He remembereth that we are but dust; He has a Creator's tenderness for the sentient beings whose very feelings are His own contrivance ; He tells our flittings, He puts our tears into His bottle; He notes in His book all our experiences with more than scientific interest and accuracy." All this might have been said of such a Christ. But the language of the Epistle to the Hebrews is very different. "He is not laying hold of angels, but He is laying hold of the seed of Abraham ; whence it was owing that He should be in all points made like unto His brethren, that He might become a merciful High Priest and a faithful in the things pertaining to God, to make propitiation for the sins of the people; for inasmuch as He hath suffered"[1]—it is an abiding fact of experience—"being tempted, He is able to succour" at each moment of danger, "them that are tempted."[2] "Having, therefore, a great High Priest that hath passed through the heavens, Jesus, the Son of God, let us hold fast our profession; for we have not an High Priest that cannot sympathize with our weaknesses" as they arise, "but one that hath been tempted in all points like as we are, without sin. Let us therefore come with boldness to the throne of grace, in order that we may receive mercy" for the past, "and may find grace for timely succour"[3] in the troubles of the present.

And while these observations regarding our Lord's moral experiences upon earth lead us to reliance upon His everlasting sympathy, they may also open up to us in part how His life, consummated and gathered up in the supreme self-sacrifice of His death, was a not unnatural

---

[1] $\pi\acute{\epsilon}\pi o\nu\theta\epsilon\nu$.   [2] Heb. ii. 16 foll.   [3] Heb. iv. 14 foll.

reparation for human sins. It is quite possible to believe that a reparation might have been effected out of the fertility of God's resources by some transaction in which human nature had no part. Such was not God's way. The race itself was to make due satisfaction for its faults. Disobedience to the will of God, and to the law of man's being, was the sin of Adam and of all His children. A co-extensive obedience was the rectification of the sin. He who offered that rectifying obedience was able to do so because, being at one and the same time infinitely more than man, and also as truly man as if He were nothing else but man, He was able to represent man at large, and men in particular, to perfection, and represented them not only in the obedience which would at all times have been due from the creature to the Creator, but also in that penitential obedience which had been made necessary by the sins of men. He heads the contrite return of conscience-stricken humanity to God, submitting itself willingly to any suffering by which God may be pleased to test its sincerity and persistence. And thus, "as through the disobedience of the one man, the many were constituted sinners, so also through the obedience of the One the many shall be constituted righteous;"[1] and "as by man came death, by man came also the resurrection of the dead."[2]

[1] Rom. v. 19.   [2] 1 Cor. xv. 21.

LECTURE III.

OUR LORD'S POWER UPON EARTH.

From the consideration of the development of our Lord's moral character as a Man, we pass to the subject of the power which He displayed during His earthly life.

It is often assumed, and not unnaturally, both by ancient and by modern writers, that in His miracles our Saviour was exercising His Divine power, and in His sufferings the weakness of the creaturely nature which He had vouchsafed to assume. He was thus alternately acting in two capacities, if I may use such an expression. He interrupted from time to time the exhibition of His Divine energy, in order to give His humanity its turn; or He interrupted the normal homeliness of a human life by wondrous vindications of His Godhead. It will be our duty to see whether the Holy Scripture bears out this distribution of our Saviour's actions.

Undoubtedly, our Lord's miracles are treated as manifestations of His being more than what other men are. The first time of His performing a miracle brings this clearly before us. "Thus did Jesus," says St. John, "make a beginning of His signs[1] in Cana of Galilee, and manifested His glory, and His disciples believed in Him."[2] The words appear to be intended to refer us back to that earlier passage where the Evangelist had said, in regard to his whole experience of fellowship with Christ on earth, "The Word was made flesh, and tabernacled among us, and we beheld His glory."[3] It is as if St. John said, "I spoke before of our having lived in the contemplation of the glory of Christ; and this was the first occasion on which we saw it, and learned to believe in Him in a way in which we had not done so before, although we were disciples already. That glory was His own

---

[1] Ταύτην ἐποίησεν ἀρχὴν τῶν σημείων. [2] St. John ii. 11.
[3] St. John i. 14.

glory. It was not a glory which lighted upon Him at times from without. The glory was there before, but it had not been manifested to us. The mighty work which He did at Cana brought it within our observation, gave it a visible expression, forced it upon our eyes. The making of the water wine showed us what was in Him. It burst upon us as a revelation of what lay beneath that quiet and simple exterior. He manifested His glory."

But it will be noticed that St. John does not say, "He manifested His Divine nature," or the like. The glory which Christ then displayed as He had never displayed it before, was not merely the possession of marvellous powers of His own. There was about that first miracle, as well as in the whole life which it illustrated, a more subtle and remarkable character than that of mere power, however great. It revealed a relationship. "We beheld His glory," says the Evangelist, in the earlier passage to which I have referred, and adds—not, as in our Old Version, "the glory as of the Only-begotten of the Father"—but, "glory as of an only-begotten come to represent a Father."[1] While the glory was indeed our Saviour's own, which He could not fail to bear about with Him, inseparable from His person, whether perceived by men or not, it was a glory which carried the thoughts of a spiritual observer back to another than the Saviour Himself. The more it was exhibited, the more the disciples felt that it told them of an unique connexion between their Master and God. That was the special feature which struck them in Christ's career—alike in its mighty deeds and in its ordinary tenor. It did not exactly strike them that He was Himself possessed of the Divine attributes, for this they did not recognise at first, and only came to believe it distinctly after His resurrection, but that the Father was manifested through Him in a sense in which no one else could manifest Him. They saw in Him "an only begotten from a Father."

That which the Evangelist propounds in this pregnant statement of the impression left upon him and his fellow-disciples by the life of our Lord, is brought out again and again by our

[1] Δόξαν ὡς μονογενοῦς παρὰ πατρός.

Lord Himself when speaking of His own actions. Although He does not treat His miracles as the highest of His credentials, but lays stress rather upon the convincing force of His teaching, yet He appeals often to the witness of His works; and it is always to establish the same truth—not His personal Godhead, although He leaves us in no doubt about His personal Godhead—but, more than that, it is to establish His unique relationship to God, to the Father. He says to Philip: "Believest thou that I am in the Father and the Father in Me? The words that I speak unto you, I speak not from Myself; but the Father, abiding in Me, doeth His works. Believe Me that I am in the Father, and the Father in Me; but if not, because of the works themselves believe."[1] To the Jews who were ready to stone Him, He says, "Many works did I show you—beautiful works—from the Father. . . . If I do not the works of My Father, believe Me not; but if I do, even if ye believe not Me, believe the works: that ye may know and go on knowing that the Father is in Me,

[1] St. John xiv. 10 foll.

and I in the Father."[1] It is always the same, "If I had not done among them the works that none other did, they had not had sin, but now they have both seen and hated both Me and My Father."[2] "The witness that I have is greater than John; for the works which the Father hath given Me that I should accomplish them, the very works that I do, bear witness concerning Me that the Father hath sent Me."[3] "The works which I do in the name of My Father, these bear witness concerning Me."[4] It is "the works of God" which are to be "manifested" in the man who was born blind.[5] The miracles are never appealed to in Scripture, unless I am greatly mistaken, as a proof of Christ's Divinity —unless, perhaps, you except St. Paul's reference to the great miracle of the Resurrection;[6] they are appealed to as a proof of that which is at once less and more than His Divinity—that is, of Christ's profound and unvarying correspondence with the Father. It was the one thing

---

[1] St. John x. 32, 37 foll.
[2] St. John xv. 24.
[3] St. John v. 36.
[4] St. John x. 25.
[5] St. John ix. 3.
[6] Rom. i. 4.

which Christ would not suffer—to allow men to suppose that His miracles had no source beyond Himself. "I am come in the name of My Father, and ye receive Me not; if another shall come in his own name, him ye will receive."[1] He did not say, "If I had come in My own name," because the thing was so inconceivable; but it is nevertheless true, that our Lord's claims would have met with less opposition amongst the Jews if He had said nothing about His Father, and had allowed them to see in His miracles only a proof of His own personal greatness.

But we may go further, and say that this rule applies not only to what we call the miraculous acts of Christ, but to His whole incarnate life. Many of the sentences which I have already quoted refer not only to miraculous acts, but to other works as well. Our Lord does not single out a particular class of His actions as proving His intimate union with the Father. He gives us to understand that every movement which He makes in life is the outcome of that union, and that there is no movement in the

[1] St. John v. 43.

Father's life which His own does not faithfully reflect, in historic succession, upon earth. "Verily, verily, I say unto you, it is impossible for the Son to do of Himself anything at all, unless he behold the Father doing aught; for whatsoever *He* doeth, these things also the Son doeth in like manner. For the Father loveth the Son, and showeth Him all things which He Himself doeth; and greater works than these will He show Him, that ye may marvel."[1] "I cannot do anything of Myself."[2] "When ye have lifted up the Son of Man, then shall ye know that I am, and that I do nothing of Myself, but as My Father taught Me, I speak these things."[3] In such words our Lord is not saying that it would have been impossible for Him to perform His *miracles* without the Father. He is teaching men that His most ordinary actions correspond with the will of His Father. The Incarnation has made no breach in that fundamental law of the being of God, that the Father and the Son do not and cannot act irrespective of each other. Although the conditions of the

[1] St. John v. 19 foll.   [2] St. John v. 30.   [3] St. John viii. 28.

Son's life are so altered by His coming down from Heaven, yet it is still the necessity of His very existence—a necessity which is His highest joy and glory—to be at all times and in every circumstance the supreme and only perfect exponent of Another.

Thus we see that, while all the actions of Christ—even the lowliest—are treated as revelations of the character and mind of the Father, and (naturally) the miraculous actions among others, none of the actions, not even the miraculous, are treated as showing that our Lord Himself was using Divine omnipotence as inherent in His own Person. He was using Divine omnipotence, indeed, but Holy Scripture represents Him as using it inherent in the person of Another with whom He was in the most perfect and indissoluble union.[1]

---

[1] See Westcott *Hebrews* p. 66 : "It is unscriptural, though the practice is supported by strong patristic authority, to regard the Lord during His historic life as acting now by His human and now by His Divine Nature only. The two natures were inseparably combined in the unity of His Person. In all things He acts personally; and, as far as it is revealed to us, His greatest works during His earthly life are wrought by the help of the Father, through the energy of a humanity enabled to do all things in fellowship with God (comp. St. John xi. 41 foll.)."

The language of our Saviour in this respect is reiterated by His Apostles. The speeches of St. Peter in the Acts are especially bold and plain in their presentment of the case. "Jesus the Nazarene," he cries on the day of Pentecost, "a Man displayed on the part of God towards you (ἄνδρα ἀποδεδειγμένον ἀπὸ τοῦ Θεοῦ εἰς ὑμᾶς), by mighty deeds and wonders and signs which God did through Him in the midst of you."[1] And lest any one should suppose that this way of looking at the miracles of Christ belonged only to the very earliest days of our dispensation, when men might still be supposed in a sense to know Christ only "after the flesh," we find St. Peter saying precisely the same thing at a later date, in his catechetical instruction of Cornelius; "Jesus which was of Nazareth, how God anointed Him with Holy Ghost and power; who went about doing good and healing all those who were oppressed by the devil, because God was with Him."[2] It would be hard to make such language fit in with the common theory that the miracles

[1] Acts ii. 22.   [2] Acts x. 38.

were the exercise of Christ's Divine nature, as the sufferings were of His humanity. We should in that case have read something more like this: "Jesus of Nazareth, a Man who displayed Himself to you as more than man, by mighty deeds and wonders and signs which He did among you;" "Jesus of Nazareth, how from His birth He possessed the fulness of the Holy Spirit and power; who went about doing good and healing all that were oppressed by the devil, because He was Himself God." No Christian can suppose for an instant that St. Peter thought of our Lord as a mere man, or that the author of the Acts intended to represent him as thinking so; yet, so far as those particular words go, they would require less violence to accommodate them to such a supposition than to the supposition that our Lord in His miracles was drawing upon His own personal resources.

It is of great interest in this connexion to endeavour to work out in the Bible the use of the word "power" and similar words in reference to our Lord's life upon earth. He is, indeed, spoken of as exercising vast power. "We were not following cunningly devised fables," says St. Peter, "when we made known to you the power and presence of our Lord Jesus Christ, but had been eye-witnesses of His majesty."[1] "Power went forth from Him," says St. Luke, "and healed all."[2] Our Lord was conscious of "power having gone forth" from Him.[3] Men came to Him saying, "If Thou wilt, Thou *canst* make me clean;"[4] and He did not repudiate the suggestion, but, on the contrary, healed the leper as of His own bounty and power: "I will; be thou clean." In keeping with this expression, He is said to have "bestowed on many that were blind the gift of sight."[5] To others, before healing them, He Himself put the question, "Do ye believe that I *can* do this?"[6] When a poor man, sickened by failures, cried to Him in despair, "If Thou *canst* do anything, have mercy upon

---

[1] 2 Peter i. 16. Doubts concerning the authorship of the Epistle do not invalidate its canonical authority.
[2] St. Luke vi. 19.   [3] St. Luke viii. 46.   [4] St. Matt. viii. 2.
[5] St. Luke vii. 21: ἐχαρίσατο βλέπειν.   [6] St. Matt. ix. 28.

us and help us,"[1] Jesus, according to the true reading, replied with a stern rebuke, Τὸ εἰ δύνῃ; ("If Thou *canst?*"), as if indignant at the suggestion that power might be wanting.

And yet there are not many passages in the Gospels which speak directly of our Lord's "power." The word "power" does not occur, for instance, in St. John. I believe I have mentioned all the passages which speak of His "power" upon earth, except one or two which offer food for serious reflexion, as seeming to indicate limitations within which He was pleased to exercise this power: "He could do no mighty work there, save that He laid His hands upon a few sick folk, and healed them: and He marvelled because of their unbelief."[2] In the very passage where He resents the imputation of the possibility of His power failing, He does not pursue simply, "All things are possible to Me;" He conditions the exercise of His power (on the common interpretation) by the faith of those on whose behalf He is to work: "If Thou canst? All things are possible to him that believeth."[3]

[1] St. Mark ix. 22. [2] St. Mark vi. 5. [3] St. Mark ix. 23.

And there is one hard phrase in St. Luke's Gospel which might appear to suggest that our Lord's exercise of miraculous power was not conditioned only by the presence or absence of faith on the part of the recipients of His bounty; nor even exclusively by the will of our Blessed Lord Himself. "It came to pass on one of those days, that He was teaching, and there were sitting by Pharisees and doctors of the law who were come out of every village of Galilee and Judæa and Jerusalem; and there was a power of the Lord that He should heal."[1] It looks as if in this passage we were to take "the Lord" in the Old Testament sense,—not referring, as it usually does in the New Testament, to the person of Christ Himself, but more generally to the covenant God of Israel. But whether it is to be referred to Christ or to the Father, the special mention of the existence of a power for healing on that occasion seems to indicate that the very power was not always present, or not always present to an equal

---

[1] St. Luke v. 17: Καὶ δύναμις Κυρίου ἦν εἰς τὸ ἰᾶσθαι αὐτόν. It seems unnatural to make αὐτόν refer to the same subject as Κυρίου.

degree. Sometimes, if the power was present, its exercise was hindered by men's want of faith; sometimes, if we rightly understand St. Luke, the power itself, according to "the Lord's" good pleasure, was withdrawn, or less freely extended.

There is another word, which, to the English reader's great loss, has been too often confounded with the word δύναμις, or "power," which is frequently used of our Blessed Lord on earth, and which throws light upon the source and nature of the power which He exercised. It is the word ἐξουσία, or "authority." It would not, indeed, be true to affirm that authority is always power delegated; for "authority" is predicated of Him to whom no delegation from another is possible. "It is not for you to know times and seasons, which the Father hath put in His own authority."[1] Neither is authority always distinguished from power as being power lawfully enjoyed — a rightful power. The Bible even speaks of turning men "from the authority of Satan" (if such an expression may stand) "unto God."[2]

[1] Acts i. 7.   [2] Acts xxvi. 18.

The distinction is rather between the inward force or faculty, which is a part of the very being of him who has "power," and the external relationship, by virtue of which one thing is superior to another, and able to command it.

In hearing and seeing the life of Jesus, men were not struck only with the inexhaustible force which sprang up within Him—though this, no doubt, struck them;—they were struck rather with the secure position of superiority in which He stood to men, and things. "The multitudes were astonished at His doctrine; for He taught them as having authority, and not as their scribes."[1] "His word was with authority."[2] "They were all amazed, so that they strove together, saying, 'What is this? a new doctrine! With authority He commandeth even the unclean spirits, and they obey Him.'"[3] "What word is this, that with authority and power"—here St. Luke combines the two words—"He commandeth the unclean spirits, and they come out!"[4]

[1] St. Matt. vii. 29.
[2] St. Luke iv. 32.
[3] St. Mark i. 27.
[4] St. Luke iv. 36.

But a position of authority naturally suggests inquiry about the origin and legitimacy of that authority; and the question, "By what authority doest Thou these things?" leads to the question, "And who gave Thee this authority?"

And here our Lord and the Evangelists leave us in no doubt. After a signal exhibition of the "authority" of "the Son of Man" in the moral and in the physical order at once, the multitude goes away "fearing, and glorifying God, which had given such authority unto men."[1] When the Son looks back upon His original mission to the world, and speaks of the world-wide authority with which He was then invested, He ascribes it, not to His own Divine nature, but to the Father's disposal: "Glorify Thy Son, that the Son may glorify Thee, according as Thou gavest Him authority over all flesh, that He should give eternal life to all that Thou hast given Him."[2] It is the same after the Resurrection, and in regard to a wider empire: "All authority was given unto Me in heaven and in earth."[3] Nay, even with

[1] St. Matt. ix. 8. [2] St. John. xvii. 2. [3] St. Matt. xxviii. 18.

reference to the Resurrection itself—the greatest of the miracles of our Lord—the one thing of which He says that He does it "of Himself,"[1]— that Resurrection of which He said in a parable, "Destroy this temple, and in three days I will raise it up,"[2]—not only does the general usage of Scripture ascribe that Resurrection directly to the Father, but in the very place where Christ says that He effects it, and the death which led to it, "of Himself," He carries His disciples back to the "authority" by which He does it. "I lay down My life, in order that I may take it again. No man took it from Me, but I lay it down of Myself. I have authority to lay it down, and I have authority to take it again. This commandment I received from My Father."[3]

While, therefore, all our Saviour's actions upon earth, miraculous and ordinary, reveal uninterruptedly the Father with whom He was one, and while the miraculous actions reveal the highest degree of power and authority bestowed upon Him for His redeeming work, we have

[1] St. John x. 18. [2] St. John ii. 19. [3] St. John x. 18.

as yet seen nothing in Scripture which would compel us to regard His miracles as wrought by virtue of His own intrinsic Godhead. There are many things which point in an opposite direction, besides those speeches of St. Peter on which we have already touched, which tell us that it was God who did Christ's miracles by means of Him. There are many things which lead us to suppose that the miraculous powers lodged in the Incarnate Son were an enrichment of His human nature, in its faithful maintenance of a right creaturely dependence upon God and obedience to Him.

Thus the miracles of our Lord are traced to the operation of the Holy Ghost. No miracle was wrought by Him before the Baptism, which was also His definite Unction to the Messiahship. There would seem to be no satisfactory reason for this, if all the miracles after His Baptism were but exhibitions of a nature which He assuredly had from the beginning. But we are not left to conjecture. "And Jesus, full of the Holy Spirit," says St. Luke, "returned from the Jordan; . . . returned in the power of the

Spirit into Galilee." His first discourse at Nazareth was an application to Himself of the prophecy, "The Spirit of the Lord is upon Me; because He hath anointed Me to preach the gospel to the poor,"[1] and so on,—a passage which does not indeed refer only to the miracles, but which at least includes them. In like manner St. Matthew applies to our Lord's miracles, and to the quiet way in which they were done, the prophecy, "Behold My servant, whom I have chosen. . . . I will put My Spirit upon Him, and He shall declare judgment to the Gentiles."[2] In the same chapter of St. Matthew, our Lord says explicitly, "If I by the Spirit of God cast out devils, no doubt the kingdom of God is come upon you,"[3] and treats the calumnies that were heaped upon His gracious miracles as blasphemy, not against Himself, but "against the Holy Ghost."[4] It would hardly seem natural to use such expressions if the miracles wrought by Christ were the outcome of His personal Godhead; they

---

[1] St. Luke iv. 1, 14. 18.
[2] St. Matt. xii. 18.
[3] St. Matt. xii. 28
[4] St. Matt. xii. 35.

are regarded as the outcome of the connexion between the Holy Ghost and His most sacred humanity.

Once more, our Blessed Lord, so far from giving us to understand that His own miracles stand on an unique footing, incommunicably His alone, speaks of them as if other men might in some sense share them, and even outstrip them. "We," He says, according to the best reading —and it is but seldom that our Lord says "We"—"We must work the works of Him that sent Me, while it is day."[1] And in another place: "Verily, verily, I say unto you, He that believeth in Me, the works that I do shall he do also; and greater than these shall he do; because I go unto the Father."[2] And once more: "Verily, I say unto you, If ye have faith, and doubt not, ye shall not only do the miracle of the fig-tree, but if ye shall even say to this mountain, Be thou removed and cast into the sea, it shall be done; and all things whatsoever ye shall ask in prayer, believing, ye shall receive."[3]

[1] St. John ix. 4.   [2] St. John xiv. 12.   [3] St. Matt. xxi. 21 f.

Our Lord seems thus to invite comparison between the miracles which He did upon earth, and those done by servants of God before and since. The difference does not seem to be that His were more in number than those done by a Moses or an Elisha, a St. Peter, or St. Paul. They probably were actually more in number; but even a great numerical excess would hardly prove that His miracles were done by inherent powers of His own, while Moses and St. Peter did theirs in the power of God. Nor is the difference that His were of a more startling and inexplicable kind than theirs. To turn all the waters of Egypt into blood was as startling and inexplicable as to turn the water at Cana into wine. To make an axehead of iron float to the surface of the river was as strange as to walk, and to make another man walk, upon the sea. The difference does not seem even to have lain—or, at any rate, not altogether—in the way in which the object was achieved. If our Lord "gives" sight to the blind, as from His own wealth and benevolence, St. Peter says to the lame man at the temple, "Such as I have, give I thee: in the name of Jesus of Nazareth, rise up and walk."[1] Christ seems clearly to indicate that His own miracles were the achievements of faith and prayer, like those of others. He looks up to heaven before He heals.[2] "Father," He cries, before His last great miracle, "I thank Thee that Thou hast heard Me."[3] Perhaps His words just quoted, about the fig tree and the mountain, are intended to imply that if the disciples would work miracles like their Master's, they must imitate His undoubting faith, and make their requests known in prayers like His. Perhaps, in His reply to the father of the lunatic child, He meant not only, "All things are possible to thee if thou believest," but also, "All things are possible to Me, because I believe." There was a great difference between our Saviour's miracles and those of Old Testament saints, and to a less extent between those which He did Himself upon earth and those greater works which apostolic men did, by His power, after He was gone; but the difference was not in the number, nor in the

---

[1] Acts iii. 6. [2] St. Mark vii. 34; cp. vi. 41. [3] St. John xi. 41.

wonderfulness, nor altogether in the method or rationale of them. It was in the spiritual teaching which they conveyed; in the moral character which they revealed; in the mind and will which prompted them. The miracles in the Acts are evidences of a spiritual power which is unsurpassed in the Gospels; but it is perhaps allowable to discern in them a falling off from the delicacy and the rich suggestiveness of those recorded to have been wrought by Christ Himself.[1]

This brings us to a point in which it may, perhaps, be said that the mode of operation—or the rationale, as I called it just now—of our Blessed Redeemer's miracles differed from that of the miracles of all other servants of God. Our Redeemer stood, by His very nature, in a

[1] "Infinitely as [the miracles of Christ] transcended the natural powers of man, they did not go beyond the powers which may supernaturally be bestowed upon man. For He Himself declares that the Apostles should not only do such works as He had done, but greater works. There is nothing, in their nature or their degree, to determine whether they were wrought by the proper power of the Divine Word, or by power bestowed upon the Incarnate Word" (Bishop O'Brien's *Charge* p. 105. The Bishop goes on to say that Scripture affords us "ample means" of determining in favour of the latter view).

unique relationship, not only with God, but also with His fellow-men. No other saint could possibly be to mankind, or to any member of the race, what Christ was and is. I do not mean that His Divine Sonship puts an infinite distance between the saints and Him—that is self-evident; but as Son of Man also, as Second Adam, as the new Representative and Head of humanity, He occupies a position with regard to mankind and to individual men which no one can share with Him, although some may come a very little nearer to such a position than others. This fact may perhaps help to interpret certain phenomena in our Lord's miracles of healing which are not to be observed in the miraculous healings wrought by others.

It has been sometimes attempted to show that while our Lord's miracles were wrought with the utmost ease and certainty, the miracles of other men cost them anxiety and effort. Elijah and Elisha stretch themselves upon the dead boy, put hand on hand and mouth on mouth, rise and walk to and fro in the house to recover energy for a fresh effort in their wrestling with death.

But Christ simply stands and says to the dead maiden, "Talitha cumi," and the maid arises; to the dead young man at Nain, "Young man, I say unto thee, Arise," and he sits up and begins to speak. It is certainly a remarkable contrast; but before we can be sure that we understand it rightly, we must look at other cases which present another aspect of Christ's power of healing. One day, when He was about to heal a deaf man in private, those few who were present, and could hear what the man to be healed could not hear, observed our Lord sigh, as He looked up to heaven, before He spoke His irresistible "Ephphatha."[1] Another day a strange inward distress seized Him, as He went, confident of the issue, to raise a friend from a four days' death; He wept, He "troubled Himself" as if by a voluntary act, He "groaned," and "again groaned within Himself," whatever may be the exact meaning of the strange word.[2] When He had absolved the sins of a palsied man whom He was expected to cure of his palsy, He replied to the cavillers by asking,

[1] St. Mark vii. 34. [2] St. John xi. 33, 35, 38.

"Whether is easier, to say, Thy sins be forgiven thee, or to say, Arise and walk?"[1] as if suggesting that neither benefit could be conferred without cost. As He passes through a crowd, a woman touches His garment and is made whole of her disease. Christ becomes aware of what has been done, by experiencing some corresponding sensation in Himself. "Somebody hath touched Me, for I perceive that virtue is gone out of Me."[2] And St. Matthew tells us of a certain evening when they brought to Him, at Capernaum, a great number of persons suffering from various ailments, and Jesus "cast out the devils with a word;" and he "healed all those who were ill." There was no failure—apparently no difficulty. It was an unparalleled exhibition of mastery over mental and physical disease. But, whether it was that our Lord explained the matter afterwards to His disciples, or whether it was that their affectionate eyes saw something that others did not see, the Evangelist remarks upon what he probably witnessed that evening in person that this was done "that it might

[1] St. Matt. ix. 5.   [2] St. Luke viii. 46.

be fulfilled which was spoken by Esaias the prophet, saying, 'He took our sicknesses Himself, and bare our diseases.'"[1]

These words do not suggest the thought of one who went about healing right and left by a mere fiat of Divine power. They point rather to an identification of the Son of Man with men which overpassed the very bounds of personality, and established a community, a solidarity (if the word may be used) between Him and them, whereby their sickness was merged in His unalterable health, and at an unimaginable cost to Him they are made whole out of His grief.

I would repeat here what I said in the first lecture, that my object is not to put forth a theory, but rather to collect the facts on which others may form theories if they please; but I believe that I have not overlooked at any rate any large body of Scriptural data which would tend to a different conclusion; and I confess that to my mind it is more attractive,

[1] St. Matt. viii. 17. St. Matthew was at Capernaum at the time.

as well as more loyal to the language of the Gospels, instead of supposing Christ to have walked the earth in constant exercise of His own Divine powers, to think of the Incarnate Son as undergoing for our sake the double self-sacrifice—not only refusing, as has been often said, to use His Divine omnipotence for His own advantage, but also refusing to use it even for ours,—preferring rather to work out our restoration by the toilsome and far-reaching exertions and sufferings of His human body and soul and spirit, in reliance upon Another who is our Father and His Father, His God as well as our God.

Indeed, if we are to look anywhere in the Incarnate life for a display of the forces of Christ's Divine personality, perhaps we may rightly look for it in the very opposite direction from that in which Christians have often looked. Instead of looking at His mighty deeds, perhaps we should think rather of His mighty sufferings. I do not mean, of course, to suggest that the Godhead in Christ became passible—although the doctrine that Godhead must be incapable of suffering is more a doctrine of the philosophers than of the Bible. But if ever there was a moment in which the weakness of His human nature seems to have been upheld and reinforced by the inexhaustible strength of His Divinity, it was, perhaps, during those three hours on the Cross, at the end of which He cried that He had been forsaken. Assuredly the forces which then upheld Him, whether to be found in His own inward depths, or in the succours of the God of whose apparent absence He complained, did not come in to neutralise the sufferings or to lift Him out of them. Quite the contrary, they lent themselves, as it were, to extend indefinitely the capacity of the human nature for realising every element in the suffering. They enabled Him to bear more, and longer, and to reach deeper and deeper into the mystery of sin. Other miracles of Christ's life, like the miracles of the prophets, might have been those of a man in complete harmony with God; the miracle of the Atoning Passion seems to me to be the one which comes nearest to being the miracle of the Divine Personality itself.

LECTURE IV.

OUR LORD'S KNOWLEDGE UPON EARTH—
APPEARANCES OF LIMITATION.

IN the last two lectures, I endeavoured to collect and arrange, as far as lay in my power, the phenomena set before us in Holy Scripture with regard to the development of our Lord's human character, and with regard to the power displayed by Him during His life on earth. It is possible that the facts, so collected and arranged, may have seemed to some of my hearers to wear an aspect to which they were unaccustomed. Nevertheless, it is our duty to examine facts, and not to shrink from them. At any rate, gentlemen, you will believe that the attempt has been made honestly and impartially. Had I known of any facts recorded in Scripture which would have put a different complexion upon the result, I should certainly have mentioned them; but I know of none. Nor need we have any fears in following the exact guidance of the Bible. We are safe, and the honour of our Lord is safe, in the hands of those who were moved by the Holy Ghost to write of Him in the first days of the Church.[1] Nothing that is found in Scripture will shake our belief in the fulness of Christ's eternal Godhead, to which all the Scriptures bear witness; and it is only so much pure gain, if by new studies, and comparing of Scripture with Scripture, we are led to realise more distinctly that His humanity is no less full and true than His Divinity.

When we pass on to consider the phenomena

[1] "It is to Scripture, not to reason, that we must look for the knowledge that will enable us either to affirm or to deny with any degree of confidence in the case. I believe, indeed, that the longer and the more deeply that it is considered independently of Scripture, the deeper and the more hopelessly inscrutable will the mystery appear. . . . Modest minds must be thoroughly convinced that their safest and wisest course is to return to Scripture, and to rest satisfied with the information which it gives on this mysterious subject" (Bishop O'Brien's *Charge* p. 35).

of the Knowledge displayed by our Lord in His earthly sojourn, we have a more difficult task to deal with than that which we attempted in my last lecture. It is not hard to conceive of power possessed but unused. Experience presents abundant examples of such a thing. We can readily think of an Almighty person choosing to perform a beneficent task by methods other than those of omnipotence. But it is much harder to bring ourselves even to entertain such a question as this — whether one who knows can voluntarily exclude his knowledge from consciousness, and only gradually win it back for himself by a process of learning?

There are many who think it impossible that our Lord, in becoming man, should have done this,—should have shut out from His life on earth that knowledge of all things temporal as well as eternal which necessarily belonged to Him as God. Among those who maintain that He did not, there are some who hold that He was simultaneously omniscient and ignorant, knowing all things as God at the same moment of time that humanly He knew nothing.[1] There are others who hold that even in His human nature Christ cannot be said to have been at any time really ignorant of anything. St. Cyril of Alexandria frankly adopts the view that our Lord only appeared to be ignorant of some things, in order to avoid a seeming incongruity between His bodily weakness and His Divine knowledge.[2] The modern Jesuit theology seems to deny even the appearance of ignorance. "The human nature," says Hurter, the most trusted living dogmatist among the Jesuits, "was subject to the general or common weaknesses of human nature; it could die; it could suffer various disadvantages, such as fatigue, and so forth, with the exception of those which carry a look of impropriety, such as ignorance."[3]

[1] "When it is said that, at one and the same time, He knew . . . as the Word, but was ignorant . . . as Man; or that while He knew . . . as regarded His Divine Nature, He was ignorant . . . as regarded His Human Nature; or that His Divine Nature knew . . . , but His Human Nature was ignorant . . .; we are in reality, though not in words, supposing Him to be made up of two Persons" (Bishop O'Brien *op. cit.* p. 104). This is Theodoret's error.
[2] See (e.g.) *Quod unus sit Christus* p. 760, Aubert.
[3] *Theol. Dogm. Compendium* ii. p. 364.

Our task is to examine and marshal the facts, not to frame an *a priori* doctrine; but this may be premised—namely, that all Christ's knowledge, as conveyed to us in the Gospel teaching, was, in its form, human knowledge, not Divine. This may sound strange; but it will be easier to grasp if we distinguish clearly between the source of His knowledge and its form. Before knowledge which was Divine in its origin could come through Him to us, it must needs be translated into human knowledge, by passing through His human mind, expressed by His human lips in human language. If, during His life on earth, He had a Divine form of knowledge along with a human form, such Divine form of knowledge must be beyond our powers of discernment. The knowledge which is available for us may be Divine in its origin, but is human in its form.

We are then to consider what is told us concerning this human knowledge of the Incarnate Word; and to-day we will consider such indications as may be alleged in favour of thinking that it was not an altogether unlimited knowledge.

Now there is, first of all, a very difficult text to be considered, in which our Lord seems, in express terms, to declare Himself to be ignorant upon a certain point. It is, of course, the saying, "But concerning that day or that hour none knoweth, —no, not the angels in heaven, nor yet the Son, —except the Father."[1] To discuss the history of the interpretation of this text would require a lecture to itself, and I shall not attempt to describe how it has been understood by various writers, ancient and modern. The Arians naturally seized upon it, and asserted on the strength of it that Christ was essentially inferior to God. The replies of Catholic apologists vary greatly in spiritual depth, in acuteness, and even (it must be confessed) in candour. Probably, however, the largest consensus of opinion would prove to be in favour of supposing that our Lord acknowledges a real ignorance on His own part with regard to this one matter—that ignorance being incident to

[1] St. Mark xiii. 32.

His temporary humiliation, and affecting only His human mind, not His Divine nature.

If we study the text closely, we see that the Authorised Version (not that it makes very much difference) creates somewhat more of a climax in the sentence than the original quite warrants. The Greek is οὐδεὶς οἶδεν, "none knoweth," quite generally; there is no express triple ascent, from men to angels, from angels to the Son. The οὐδεὶς οἶδεν includes all that follows, and would naturally have led on at once to εἰ μὴ ὁ πατήρ, "none knoweth, except the Father;" but then, to strengthen the negation, and practically to induce the disciples to be content with their ignorance, our Lord inserts the words which tell them that the universal ignorance which He has predicated is indeed universal, and not human only — including beings above mankind, as well as man. "None knoweth—no, not the angels in heaven, nor yet the Son—except the Father." All the same, the sentence *is* a climax, and a pointed one. Our Lord does not say (what would have been good Greek) οὐδὲ οἱ ἄγγελοι οὔτε ὁ υἱός, as if the Son were in the same class of beings with the angels in heaven, only the highest of them. He says, οὐδὲ ... οὐδέ; as if to say, "You might suppose that the secret was only a secret from those on earth; but it is kept a secret even from those in heaven. You might suppose that the secret was only a secret for created beings, but it is a secret for the uncreated Son Himself. The Father alone knows it."

I confess that the more I study the passage, the less satisfied I am to think that our Lord is referring to Himself as conditioned by the special circumstances in which He spoke, and only then to the human part of His composite consciousness. The climax itself seems against it, especially with the words, "in heaven;" for on any showing in His human nature Christ was not yet in heaven, but was made "a little lower than the angels." We should at least have expected Him to say, "None knoweth—no, not the angels in heaven; nor even I," or, "nor even the Son of Man." This would easily have given room for the necessary gloss, confining His ignorance to His human nature, and to His passing phase of existence. If He had even said, "No, not the Son of God," there would have been something to help the interpretation. But, with all the force of a powerful climax, our Lord leads up to His most absolute and eternal title, " no, not the Son," and follows it by the absolute correlative, "except the Father."

It is impossible to look through the passages where Christ is spoken of under this absolute title without feeling that it means more here than the common interpretation allows. It is not a title which is frequently and loosely used. This is the only passage in which St. Mark uses it. The only other occasion where it occurs in the Synoptic Gospels is the solemn passage, "None knoweth the Son, but the Father; neither doth any know the Father, but the Son, and he to whomsoever the Son is pleased to reveal Him."[1] It occurs once in St. Paul: "Then shall the Son also Himself be subjected to Him that subjected all things to Him, that God may be all things in all."[2] It occurs once in the Epistle

[1] St. Matt. xi. 27; comp. St. Luke x. 22.   [2] 1 Cor. xv. 28.

to the Hebrews: "But unto the Son He saith, Thy throne, O God, is for ever and ever. . . . And Thou, Lord, in the beginning didst lay the foundation of the earth."[1] It occurs twenty-two times in the writings of St. John; and every time, as the passages which I have quoted from elsewhere would lead us to expect, the title points to the eternal and necessary relations of the persons of the Godhead, and not to anything resulting from the Incarnation. For instance, when Christ says, "The Son can do nothing of Himself,"[2] no one can suppose that He is referring to restrictions imposed upon His Divine liberties by His earthly state: He lays open the very bond which connects the Father and Himself irrespective of creation and its movements. Of course the addition of qualifying words might point us to something accidental or assumed, as, for instance, when He says, "The Father hath committed all judgment unto the Son . . . because He is Son of Man;"[3] but without those last words we should never have

[1] Heb. i. 2 foll. I take ὁ Θεός to be the vocative; but it makes little difference for the present purpose to take it otherwise.
[2] St. John v. 19.   [3] St. John v. 22, 27.

gathered that the reason why the Son is our Judge is a reason lying outside the eternal and necessary relations of the persons of the Trinity. In the same way, if Christ had said, "None knoweth, no, not the angels in heaven, nor yet the Son Himself upon earth," all would have been plain. But when He says absolutely, "nor yet the Son, but the Father," we must, I believe, see in the statement something belonging to the essential relation of Son to Father in the Godhead.

If this is so, the subject of my lectures does not demand that I should inquire further into the meaning of the text. We are investigating what is told us concerning our Lord's knowledge upon earth, not the fundamental conditions of the existence of the Eternal Son. But I will avow that if the Son says that He Himself, as Son, does not know concerning the day and hour of the Judgment, then, in spite of the remonstrances of Theodoret,[1] I must side rather with the Cyrillian interpreters, and suppose that He does not predicate of

[1] *Reprehens.* xii. *Capitum Cyrilli*, *Anathem.* 4.

Himself an absolute and entire ignorance. From what other Scriptures tell us, it is plain that whatever the Father knows, the Son knows also—and that of necessity no less than of choice. I should, therefore, be inclined to class the passage with others like "It is not Mine to give, but it shall be given to them for whom it is prepared of My Father."[1] It would imply that the cognisance of such questions as those of times and seasons, along with all other forms of predestination, lies not with created beings, nor even with the Son, as Son, but with Him alone who is the source of all thought and purpose and action, even the Father. But however the text may be interpreted, no way of interpreting it seems to my mind so full of difficulties as that which would make the date of the Judgment a solitary and designed exception to a human knowledge otherwise universal on the part of the Incarnate Lord.

Leaving this text, therefore, as not bearing directly upon our subject, let us pass to that group of texts in which there is mention of our

[1] St. Matt. xx. 23.

Lord's intellectual development. "The young Child grew, and strengthened, filling continually (πληρούμενον) with wisdom, and the grace (or favour) of God was upon Him."[1] "Jesus advanced (προέκοπτεν), in wisdom and stature and grace (or favour) with God and men."[2] With these words of the Gospel, describing the sacred childhood and youth respectively, we may set once more a passage of prophecy on which we have touched before. "The Lord God hath given Me the tongue of the scholar, that I should know how to speak a word in season to him that is weary: He wakeneth (*i.e.* teacheth) morning by morning, He wakeneth Mine ear to hear as the scholar."[3]

Now, it may justly be said that these texts do not deal definitely and only with an intellectual development—not even the second, which is the *locus classicus*. St. Luke does not say, "Jesus advanced in knowledge." Wisdom is a larger thing than knowledge; and in the Bible it has a meaning which is even more distinctly ethical than mental. To advance in

[1] St. Luke ii. 40.   [2] St. Luke ii. 52.   [3] Isa. l. 4.

wisdom means much more than an increasing accumulation of facts acquired. It includes the faculty of insight and discernment, to penetrate the significance of things; and the practical sagacity which sees, from such a study of facts, what is to be done; perhaps, above all, it involves the reverent recognition of God, and His sobering and uplifting presence. St. Luke's language does not, therefore, directly teach that the Holy Child began with knowing nothing, and that the bounds of a sinless and natural ignorance retired, as He came to have a mind and memory more and more stored with truths which He had learned. Yet it cannot be disputed that the main effect of the text is to set before us the picture of a perfect development in every department of life — ethical and intellectual, physical, religious. It was the first occasion on which the world had seen a normal and sound human development — except, as the Epistle to the Hebrews sadly notes, that the normal development took place in circumstances which were *not* normal: "He learned by the things which He suffered." And however much we may admit the ethical aspect of that "wisdom" in which Jesus advanced, it cannot at any rate altogether exclude the element of knowledge in one important direction. It involves at least a growing appreciation of the ways and purposes of God to which Jesus was to devote Himself. It would impair our confidence in the accuracy of the Scriptures, as well as our sense of true fellowship with the life of the Incarnate Son, if we could suppose, with St. Cyril, in opposition to what seems to be the obvious meaning of St. Luke's language, that the human mind of the Babe of Bethlehem, of the Boy at Nazareth, was at each instant from the beginning scientifically and uniformly acquainted with every branch of knowledge, and only refrained from appearing to be so, out of respect for the feelings of those around Him.[1]

[1] "As His body grew visibly, like the bodies of other human beings, so His mind advanced also. . . . And as all this—everything connected with His humiliation—was not a show, but a reality, we must be sure that, as regards knowledge, His mind followed the ordinary law of the development of human minds, so that He knew more at a later stage of His life than at an earlier, which is the same thing as to say that He was ignorant of some things at an earlier stage of His life which He knew at a later" (Bishop O'Brien *op. cit.* p. 37).

And, we may add, the language of the Bible, in the passages now before us, does not suggest the notion of some other all-embracing form of knowledge held simultaneously in reserve. The eternal life of the Godhead is not measured out in parallel succession to our days and years; and in studying the life which the Son of God vouchsafed to live in time, we need not, perhaps, encumber ourselves with the notion of such a higher form of knowledge accompanying the development of the lower, side by side, day by day. The relation of the eternal to the temporal must remain for us unknown at present; and while we watch the progress of the earthly life of the Son of God, we are constrained to think of Him as wholly engaged in it. There, at Bethlehem now, and now at Nazareth, is His centre of personality. Although it is in virtue of His human nature, not of His Divine nature, that the Lord is the subject of growth and progress, yet it is He that advances, and that is conscious of the advance—not some outlying group of faculties remotely connected with

His real self. "Jesus advanced." It is the very personal Word of God Incarnate who thus passes from such a state of sensation, perception, knowledge, as belongs to the embryo, the babe, the child, relatively perfect in each stage, to that of the full-grown man, of the complete head of the race, "to the measure of the stature of the fulness of the Christ."

Having thus seen that the knowledge of the Incarnate Son was a progressive and increasing knowledge during the years of His youthful evolution, we will now note such phrases as seem to indicate that, even in later days, He continued— if I may reverently say so—to live and learn, as other men do,—that is, to pass from a less to a more complete acquaintance with facts.

It is worth while, for example, to look at some of the many places in the Gospels, where Jesus is said—not (as is also often said of Him) to "know" (εἰδέναι) the given state of things —but to "come to know," or "perceive" (γνῶναι), or the like.[1]

---

[1] See Westcott's notes on St. John ii. 25, especially the Additional Note.

The Pharisees take counsel to destroy Him. At first, it seems to be implied, He was unaware of it; for "when Jesus came to know, He withdrew Himself from thence."[1] Rumours reach the Pharisees with regard to the relative success of John the Baptist and of our Lord's disciples, and stir much discussion among them. Intelligence of these discussions is conveyed to our Lord: "When, therefore, the Lord came to know that the Pharisees had heard that Jesus was making and baptizing more disciples than John, . . . He left Judæa and went away back into Galilee."[2] Plots, ostensibly for His honour, are formed among the five thousand whom He had miraculously fed. "Jesus, therefore, having come to know that they were about to come and seize Him to make Him king, withdrew again into the mountain alone by Himself."[3] A man has been bedridden for thirty-eight years, when one day our Lord comes to the pool by which he lies. There is nothing to show that our Lord went to the pool for the purpose of

[1] St. Matt. xii. 15.   [2] St. John iv. 1, 3.   [3] St. John vi. 15.

healing him, or had thought of him before; but when He arrived, "Jesus, seeing this man lie, and coming to know"—we are not informed how, but perhaps by miraculous insight—"that he had now been a long time in that case," proceeded to heal him.[1]

In these instances, the new knowledge acquired dictates fresh action; in many others it suggests a speech or a question. Our Lord discovers that the disciples are grossly misinterpreting a metaphor of His: "And when He came to know it, He saith to them, Why reason ye because ye have no loaves?"[2] They are perplexed over another dark saying of His, and after fruitless discussions among themselves, reluctantly acquiesce in not understanding. "Jesus came to know that they wished to ask Him, and said unto them, Do ye inquire among yourselves of that I said?"[3] When the scribes murmured at the absolution of the palsied man, "Jesus immediately became fully aware in His spirit (εὐθὺς ἐπιγνοὺς τῷ πνεύματι αὐτοῦ) that they were thus reasoning

---

[1] St. John v. 6.   [2] St. Mark viii. 17.   [3] St. John xvi. 19.

APPEARANCES OF LIMITATION. 133

among themselves, and said, Why reason ye these things in your hearts?"[1] About the tribute question, "Jesus, coming to know, or perceiving (γνούς), their wickedness, said, Why tempt ye Me, ye hypocrites?"[2] The disciples murmur at Mary's waste of ointment: "Jesus, coming to know it, said to them, Why trouble ye the woman?"[3] Such passages seem to show that our Saviour's knowledge of things around Him was, like ours, discursive, coming to Him at successive moments, and not exhaustive from the outset and therefore stationary; in other words, that He was aware of a thing at one instant, of which He was not aware the instant before.

Sometimes these moments at which our Lord became aware, or more vividly aware, of a thing are recorded to have occasioned in Him a rising of holy passion. All passion implies a kind of access of knowledge or, at any rate, of realisation; and a being to whom everything is fully and unincreasably known and felt, would seem to be thereby precluded

[1] St. Mark ii. 8.   [2] St. Matt. xxii. 18.   [3] St. Matt. xxvi. 10.

from passion. Thus, on the disciples trying to keep back the children from Him, "When Jesus saw it, He was indignant."[1] When the people in the synagogue maintained an obstinate silence, and would not answer His question about good works on the sabbath, "having glanced round about on them with wrath, being altogether grieved at the hardening of their heart, He saith to the man, Stretch out thy hand."[2] Sights and sounds often affected Him thus. More than once we are told that "coming forth and seeing a great multitude, He was moved with compassion."[3] It is as if He had hardly been prepared for such a spectacle. At sight of the widow at Nain, He was moved with compassion.[4] "When Jesus saw [Mary] weeping, and the Jews which came together with her weeping, He groaned in spirit" (with indignant emotion), "and troubled Himself."[5] When the rich young ruler professed that he had kept all the commandments, "Jesus looked upon him and loved him."[6] When "the

---

[1] St. Mark x. 14. [2] St. Mark iii. 5. [3] St. Matt. xiv. 14.
[4] St. Luke vii. 13. [5] St. John xi. 33. [6] St. Mark x. 21.

seventy returned again with joy," " in that very hour He rejoiced in the Holy Spirit, and said, I thank Thee, Father, Lord of heaven and earth."[1] In the triumphal Entry, "as He drew near, seeing the city, He wept over it."[2] Emotions evidently break forth in a similar manner on other occasions, though without the same explicit mention.

As I have said, all movements of passion imply the rushing into the mind of new thoughts. They contain an element of surprise. But it is highly significant that surprise itself, in the form of wonder, is several times predicated of our Saviour. Wonder is the shock, whether agreeable or otherwise, of the strange and unexpected. Wonder is the result of a new and significant truth being forced upon the consciousness, which cannot all at once be co-ordinated with what was known or thought before. And so we find in the life of Christ that He wondered at some men's faith, and at some men's unbelief. The people of His own country, Nazareth, among whom He had

[1] St. Luke x. 21. [2] St. Luke xix. 41.

increased in favour with God and men, might reasonably have been expected to welcome Him; and "He marvelled at their unbelief."[1] When the Jews on every side were looking askance at Him, a Gentile officer entreats Him for a word of healing, not doubting that the powers of nature will obey His command as promptly as soldiers in the ranks obey their centurion; "and when Jesus heard these things, He marvelled at him, and turning to the multitude that followed Him, He said, I tell you, I have not found so great faith, no, not in Israel."[2] And there was one terrible occasion in His life when wonder became astonishment and anguish. Ἤρξατο ἐκθαμβεῖσθαι καὶ ἀδημονεῖν—"He began to be sore amazed and very heavy."[3] Θάμβος differs from θαῦμα both in excess of volume, being an overwhelming degree of astonishment, and also as containing a suggestion of alarm: and ᾿κθαμβεῖσθαι is to go the whole length of such astonishment, and to be transported out of one's self by it. Ἀδημονεῖν denotes a kind of stupefaction and bewilderment, the intellectual

[1] St. Mark vi. 6. [2] St. Luke vii. 9. [3] St. Mark xiv. 33.

powers reeling and staggering under the pressure of the ideas presented to them. This is what the Lord vouchsafed to undergo. The transition from imagination beforehand to actual experience was more than He could well bear, and He felt that it was killing Him. "My soul is exceeding sorrowful, even unto death." It took away His spiritual breath, so that His very prayers in those long hours in the Garden were but broken ejaculations, again and again repeated, "saying the same words." Although He had come into the world for the very purpose of bearing sin; although He had long lived on earth among sinners, and feeling the hatefulness of their sins; although He had had foretastes and anticipations of Gethsemane itself, as when He cried, "Now is My soul troubled, and what shall I say?"[1] yet, when the hour came, it exceeded all His expectations. The sensation of having sin—all sin—laid upon Him as His own burden now dismayed and appalled Him, and made Him entreat, as we may well believe that He had

[1] St. John xii. 27.

never before entreated, that, if it were possible, the cup might pass from Him. And as that most awful prayer indicates that He had not fully realised beforehand what He was then experiencing, so also it seems to imply that even then He was not absolutely certain of the future. He could hardly have prayed, "If it be possible," with that reiteration and at such length, and with so heart-piercing an appeal, if it had been clear to Him all the time that there was positively no other way.

Our Blessed Lord appears, then, to have gone on acquiring knowledge during His life upon earth. And we may reverently ask, by what means that knowledge was gained. To this question different answers will naturally have to be given, according to the different departments of knowledge. We will only touch at present upon those incidents in His life where He appears to gather knowledge by the same methods which are open to all men.

Many things He knew by personal observation. "Jesus, seeing their faith, said unto the sick of the palsy."[1] "Seeing the multitudes, He was moved with compassion for them, because they were agitated and tossed about, like sheep that have no shepherd."[2] "Seeing them grievously distressed in rowing (for the wind was against them), about the fourth watch of the night, He cometh unto them."[3] "Peter took Him unto him, and began to rebuke Him; but He, turning and seeing His disciples, rebuked Peter."[4] "Jesus, seeing him that he answered discreetly, said to him, Thou art not far from the kingdom of God."[5] "While He was yet speaking, there came some from the ruler of the synagogue's house saying, Thy daughter is dead; why troublest thou the Rabbi any further? But Jesus, overhearing the word as it was uttered ($\pi\alpha\rho\alpha\kappa o\acute{u}\sigma\alpha\varsigma\ \tau\grave{o}\nu\ \lambda\acute{o}\gamma o\nu\ \lambda\alpha\lambda o\acute{u}\mu\epsilon\nu o\nu$), saith, Fear not."[6] Examples of such observation might be multiplied.

But there were other things which our Lord learned by the information of others. "Hearing that John was delivered up, He retired into

---

[1] St. Matt. ix. 2. [2] St. Matt. ix. 36. [3] St. Mark vi. 48.
St. Mark viii. 32. [5] St. Mark xii. 34. [6] St. Mark v. 36.

Galilee."[1] "His disciples took up the body and buried him, and went and informed Jesus. And when Jesus heard it, He retired thence."[2] "Jesus heard that they had cast him out; and found him, and said, Dost thou believe in the Son of Man?"[3] "They sent unto Him, saying, Lord, he whom Thou lovest is sick. . . . When, therefore, He heard that he was sick, He then abode two days in the place where He was."[4]

These occasions on which our Lord is said to have learned facts by being told them, lead us on to inquire whether He ever sought to ascertain facts by such means. The questions of Christ afford a singularly instructive field for study. As was natural in a life of full and busy intercourse with men, our Lord asked many questions; and those which are recorded are asked in various tones, and for various reasons.

The greater number of our Lord's questions in the Gospels are plainly dialectical. Like other great teachers, He was wont to draw

---

[1] St. Matt. iv. 12.
[2] St. Matt. xiv. 12 foll.
[3] St. John ix. 35.
[4] St. John xi. 3, 6.

APPEARANCES OF LIMITATION. 141

men out, and to lead them on, from what they acknowledged, to the rightful deductions. Examples of such dialectical questions, where plainly the Lord had no need to learn, but only wished to test, are the following: "Whose is this image and superscription?"[1] "Whom do men say that I, the Son of Man, am? . . . but whom say ye that I am?"[2] "Of whom do the kings of the earth take tribute? of their own children, or of strangers?"[3] "The baptism of John, was it from heaven, or of men?"[4] "What think ye concerning the Christ? whose son is he? . . . How, then, doth David in the Spirit call him Lord?"[5] "When I sent you forth without purse and scrip and shoes, lacked ye anything?"[6]

Some of this class of questions are even more rhetorical than dialectical, and indicate some degree of suprise or indignation; such as, "Art thou a master of Israel, and knowest not these things?"[7] "Did ye never read what David

[1] St. Matt. xxii. 20.
[2] St. Matt. xvi. 13 foll.
[3] St. Matt. xvii. 25.
[4] St. Matt. xxi. 25.
[5] St. Matt. xxii. 42 foll.
[6] St. Luke xxii. 35.
[7] St. John iii. 10.

did, when he was an hungred?"[1] "He looked upon them, and said, What, then, is this which is written, The stone which the builders rejected, the same is become the headstone in the corner?"[2] "Were there not ten cleansed? and where are the nine?"[3] "Simon, sleepest thou? couldest thou not watch with Me one hour?"[4]

In these places our Lord is evidently asking without any purpose of seeking information; but there is a class of questions occupying debatable ground, where it would be natural, in the case of any other than our Lord, to suppose the question to be asked for information's sake, but where, in His case, we may legitimately seek some other interpretation, and may find one without much difficulty. St. Athanasius instances one or two of these as a sign that our Lord had adopted all the sinless infirmities of our limited nature. The Arians, he says, are like the Jews, and keep saying, "How can He be the Word, or God, who, like a man, sleeps,

[1] St. Matt. xii. 3.
[2] St. Luke xx. 17.
[3] St. Luke xvii. 17.
[4] St. Mark xiv. 37.

APPEARANCES OF LIMITATION. 143

and weeps, and asks questions?"[1] "Both [Jews and Arians]," he continues, "arguing from the human conditions to which the Saviour submitted because of the flesh which He had, deny the eternity and Godhead of the Word."

One of the questions which St. Athanasius thus regards as asked by the Saviour for His human information is the question to the friends of Lazarus, "Where have ye laid him?"[2] The eleventh chapter of St. John is indeed a marvellous weaving together of that which is natural and that which is above nature. Jesus learns from others that Lazarus is sick, but knows without any further message that Lazarus is dead. He weeps and groans at the sight of the sorrow which surrounds Him, yet calmly gives thanks for the accomplishment of the miracle before it has been accomplished. In these circumstances, although there would be nothing derogatory to the Lord's dignity in ascertaining by inquiry the simple matter of fact, as St. Athanasius supposed that He did,

[1] Ath. *c. Arian*. Or. iii. 457.   [2] St. John xi. 34.

yet perhaps He was but using a natural form of speech equivalent to an invitation to go with Him to the grave.

The same kind of doubt hangs around such questions as that addressed to the blind men who asked for healing, "Believe ye that I am able to do this?"[1] as though He were not fully satisfied that the rightful conditions for healing were present; or to that other blind man who was healed by successive stages; "He asked him if he saw aught,"[2] — as though in a case where faith was apparently so imperfect, our Lord proceeded tentatively, and wished to make sure of one step before He took another. So, in a course of instruction to the disciples, he tentatively asks, "Have ye understood all these things?"[3] before closing the lesson. The questions, however, may have been asked only for the sake of the blind men, or of the disciples themselves. Take, again, the questions to the father of the demoniac child, and to the crowd assembled under the mountain of Transfiguration. "What reason ye with them

[1] St. Matt. ix. 28. [2] St. Mark viii. 23. [3] St. Matt. xiii. 51.

(*i.e.* with the disciples)?"¹ "How long a time is it since this hath been the case with him?"² The first question may be but an obvious way of opening communications, the second of expressing sympathy; though they look as if they might mean more. Jesus says to the raving man near Gerasa, "What is thy name?"³ possibly, in part, because it was an obvious way of finding out; but, doubtless, much more because it brought the poor man back to his true self, and was a first step to ridding him of the confusion of his distracted personality. "How many loaves have ye?"⁴ The exact number was practically unimportant to Him; and the addition, "Go and see," seems to make it clear that the main object of the interrogation was to impress the disciples' minds; but Christ may have been interested to learn,—and this is another of the questions adduced by St. Athanasius as exemplifying His human method of gaining knowledge. "Woman, where are those thine accusers? hath no man condemned

---

[1] St. Mark ix. 16.   [2] St. Mark ix. 21.
[3] St. Mark v. 9.   [4] St. Mark vi. 38.

thee?"[1] appears in like manner intended to impress the woman's mind; but it at least suggests some measure of surprise on the part of our Lord. "What was it that ye disputed by the way?"[2] is designed to elicit a confession; but there is additional point in it, if we might suppose that He who one day (as we have seen) "overheard" a remark in the crowd, had, on this journey, observed an eager dispute, and had surmised that there was evil in it, but had not applied Himself at the moment to apprehend the precise point of it. When He says to the mother of Zebedee's children, "What wilt thou?"[3] it is an invitation to make known her request; but if it be ever allowable to suppose that Jesus was not aware of the answer before He asked a question, it would be allowable here. His emotion at her reply, and His statement that the granting of her request did not lie in His personal option, tend rather to that view than to the opposite.

It is doubtful whether in the questions which we have just considered, our Lord is, at any rate

[1] St. John viii. 10. [2] St. Mark ix. 33. [3] St. Matt. xx. 20.

APPEARANCES OF LIMITATION. 147

in part, acquiring a knowledge of the state of the case in the same kind of way as we do, making Himself beholden to others for telling Him. But there remain a few instances in which I cannot doubt that the question, spoken or implied, denotes that the Divine questioner was not beforehand in full possession of the facts.

The earliest recorded words of Jesus form a question, and a question of surprise and perplexity. How is it that ye sought Me? Wist ye not that I must be in My Father's house?"[1] The whole incident is one which reveals to us our Saviour's perfect accommodation of Himself to the conditions of true and simple childhood. It is well-nigh impossible to believe that He knew that Joseph and Mary were leaving Jerusalem, that He knew them to be unaware of His tarrying behind, that He knew the sorrow which they were experiencing in searching for Him, and that He deliberately did what He did, for the express purpose of teaching them a lesson. Such a notion would seem to turn the exquisite narrative of St. Luke into an unedifying and almost a

[1] St. Luke ii. 49.

repulsive incident. St. Luke's language is as far from suggesting such a view as it is from suggesting that the Holy Child sat among the doctors consciously to instruct and not to learn. It can hardly be doubted that one who read these verses without a theological prepossession, would say that by some blameless accident, arranged in the providence of God, the parents had reason to suppose that the Holy Child knew of the time for the starting of the caravan, and to suppose that He was actually in it when He was not; and that He for His part—we may not say thought them to be still in Jerusalem,. for that would imply a definite error, which would be altogether unnecessary, and which nothing in the Bible would justify—but was as unconscious of their starting as if they had started while He was asleep. How soon He became aware of the fact we are not told, but doubtless very soon; and His astonished question seems, not to mean that He had expected them to know that it was His duty to stay at Jerusalem, but rather that He had expected them, on discovering their loss, to come straight for Him to the Temple—to the natural spot, from which, in His thoughtfulness, He had not stirred under any influence of fear. "How is it that ye *sought* Me? Wist ye not that I was bound to be in My Father's house?" He was as yet a stranger upon earth, and its ways, even in the actions of the saints, were a perplexity to Him. He could not make them out.

Another instance is that of the extraordinary miracle of the woman with an issue of blood. She came with the intention of obtaining, if possible, a cure by stealth. She had no desire, as it seems, to enter into any personal relations with our Lord, but to draw off a healing virtue from Him as by a magical process. And she gained her wish. There seems, from the account, to have been no exertion of will on our Lord's part to effect the cure. If we are to understand the words of the Gospel literally, He only perceived that some one had been healed by an inward sensation of having given off virtue. St. Mark's language is very remarkable: "And Jesus immediately becoming well aware in Himself (ἐπιγνοὺς ἐν ἑαυτῷ) of the virtue in Him having gone out (τὴν ἐξ αὐτοῦ δύναμιν ἐξελθοῦσαν —not τὴν ἐξελθοῦσαν ἐξ αὐτοῦ δύναμιν)." Who it was that had been healed He did not know, although He felt that it had been done by a touch—according to St. Mark's graphic account, that it had been done by a touch of His clothes. "He turned in the crowd and said," perhaps said more than once (ἔλεγεν), "Who touched My clothes?"[1] In spite of the denials and the wondering expostulations of Peter and the disciples, He persisted. "Somebody touched Me," He said, according to St. Luke;[2] "I felt virtue gone out of Me (ἔγνων δύναμιν ἐξεληλυθυῖαν);" and "He kept looking round about (περιεβλέπετο) to see the woman that had done this." It is almost impossible to suppose that all this animated and prolonged investigation was only a piece of instructive acting, in order to compel the woman to declare herself. There were indeed occasions when our Saviour used a holy pretence. "He meant to pass by them (ἤθελεν παρελθεῖν αὐτούς),"[3] when He walked on the sea; "He feigned to be travelling

[1] viii. 46. [2] St. Mark v. 30. [3] St. Mark vi. 48.

further (προσεποιήσατο),"[1] when He came with His fellow-travellers to Emmaus. But in the case before us, not only is there nothing to indicate that our Lord was feigning ignorance, —what is said of the means by which He perceived the cure to have been effected points to the conclusion that the ignorance (such as it was) was real.

Another case where it is hard to suppose our Lord to have been feigning, is the incident of the Barren Fig-tree. Our Lord was really hungry. From a distance He saw "one fig tree" covered with leaves amidst the bare, pale stems of the rest. From its forward condition it seemed to offer a promise of fruit. Our Lord asked no question; there would have been no one to answer it; but His conduct contained a question. He moved towards the tree with an inquiring gaze—possibly with a touch of surprise that any fig tree should, so early in the season, be so advanced—" He went to it, εἰ ἄρα τι εὑρήσει ἐν αὐτῇ to see if He should indeed find anything upon it."[2] That every point in the

[1] St. Luke xxiv. 28. [2] St. Mark xi. 13.

incident was Divinely purposed, in order to bring out a great spiritual lesson, cannot be doubted; but the reality of our Lord's hunger appears to show that His uncertainty as to the means of satisfying it was real also. If He only pretended not to know that the tree was barren, we should expect the hunger also to have been pretended; but an actual hunger does not match so well with a symbolical quest of nutriment.

There is only one other question of the Blessed Lord's on which I will now speak. It was the last question of His earthly life, and it was the most tremendous. His first recorded question denoted perplexity at the ways of men; His last denotes a more dreadful perplexity at the ways of God. Into the whole mystery of that cry [1]—the strangest that ever passed the lips of man—we need not now enter. How our sins were laid upon Him, and made His own, and felt by Him in such a way that He was not able to look up; how it was possible for the Son of God to feel Himself forsaken by His Father—that Father of whom

[1] St. Matt. xxvii. 46: "Eli, Eli, lama sabachthani?"

He had said so confidently, a short while before, to His disciples, "Ye shall be scattered every one to his own, and shall leave Me alone; and yet I am not alone, because the Father is with Me"[1]—this may devoutly be studied at another time. But what concerns us to-day is to see that the question is a real question, not a rhetorical question. It expresses—who can doubt it?—a longing on Christ's part for some light of understanding to illuminate the dreadful bewilderment in which He finds Himself. It shows that He knew by experience, as we do, what it is to challenge the dealings of God, and to expostulate with them,—to feel that He is in "a land of darkness, as darkness itself, and of the shadow of death, without any order, and where the light is as darkness." His "why" is as real a "why" as ours. Even if He, as is often the case with us, could give a verbal answer to His own question, yet the answer seems to leave the heart of the difficulty untouched. In view of this piercing "why," it seems unnecessary to imagine some solitary items here and there,

[1] St. John xvi. 32.

designedly excluded from an otherwise absolute and exhaustive understanding of all things. It shows us that there was one hour, one three hours, in the life of the Incarnate God when everything seemed to go from Him except trust in "His God;" and there is no other hour in His life of which the record so bows us in adoration at the feet of " Jesus, Divinest when He most is Man." [1]

[1] Myers' *Saint Paul*.

LECTURE V.

OUR LORD'S KNOWLEDGE UPON EARTH—
ITS TRANSCENDENCE.

IN my last lecture we considered the appearances of limitation in our Redeemer's knowledge while He was upon earth, as indicated in the Gospels. We saw some reasons for concluding that it was not, from His conception to the Cross, an unvarying, exhaustive, all-comprising acquaintance with all facts, great and small, in all their bearings; but that it was a progressive knowledge, as ours is, beginning with less, and advancing to more, by observation and reflexion, and by information received from others, as well as by other means; and that there were things which He perceived for the first time, and things which caused Him surprise and perplexity, sometimes even an anguish of perplexity.

But we have, to-day, to enter upon the larger subject, not of the limitations, but of the extent of Christ's knowledge; and, where that knowledge exceeds the usual bounds of human knowledge, we may endeavour to see whether Holy Scripture gives us any information as to its sources.

The Bible, which was written for our learning, but not to satisfy our curiosity, does not tell us how far our Blessed Lord was acquainted with facts such as those of natural science or of secular history; and we could only guess one way or the other, if we cared to do so. His language about the lilies and the sparrows, His parables of the Sower, the Mustard-seed, and others, show Him, as was to be expected, to have had a thoughtful and devout eye for the visible creation; and the more scientifically nature is studied, the more richly suggestive does our Lord's parabolic teaching appear: but there is no proof that He had applied His human mind to the examination of the laws of science. The absence of evidence leaves it open for us to think either way. The reference to the fall of the tower in Siloam is, so far as I remember, His only recorded mention of a public event in the past, outside of His own circle of observation on the one hand, or of Scripture history on the other. That there were in that perfect human nature capacities and tastes for scientific study and learned research cannot be questioned, as well as for music and art, and every other wholesome pursuit in which men delight; but to give time and attention to these would have interfered with the main purpose of His life, and it would seem that He sacrificed them.[1]

But while we are not informed on the points which I have named, we have plentiful proof that Christ had knowledge of facts which no ordinary study could have ascertained; and first, in the present, external order. The miracle of the fish with the stater in his mouth was such a miracle of knowledge, rather than a miracle of power. It was curious, but not necessarily miraculous, that a fish in the lake should have swallowed a stater. It was a striking instance of the Divine Providence, though

[1] St. John v. 30; cp. Godet *Études Bibliques* ii. p. 100.

not perhaps the direct act of Christ Himself, that that particular fish should take St. Peter's hook, and at that juncture. The miraculous thing was, that our Lord should know the very fishes walking in the paths of the sea, and should be able to say that that fish would be the first on St. Peter's line. And in immediate contact with that miracle of knowledge was another. The conversation between the tribute-collectors and St. Peter took place when Jesus was not present. It was somewhat rash of St. Peter to pledge his Master to the payment. "And when he" (that is, St. Peter) "came into the house" (where Jesus was), "Jesus anticipated him (προέφθασεν αὐτόν);" He did not wait for St. Peter to explain what he had done; He knew it already. After showing that He and His disciples were under no obligations of ransom to the house of His Father, He pointed him to this means of acquitting the supposed obligation for the sake of giving no scandal; "That take and give them instead of Me and thee."[1] So loftily did He reassure His disciples

[1] St. Matt. xvii. 24 foll.

again, after His second announcement of the approaching Passion.

In the same supernatural way, if I rightly understand, and not by previous arrangement, our Lord tells His two disciples of the tied ass and her unridden colt at Bethphage, and of the man bearing the pitcher of water in the city. The owner of the asses and the good-man of the house were, I doubt not, known to the Lord, if not to the Apostles, as believers; but there is no sign of anything having been preconcerted with them—rather the contrary— with regard to the use of the animals and of the chamber. And yet, in either case, the supernatural knowledge displayed by our Lord is accompanied by phenomena which carry us back to what we were reviewing in my last lecture. Our Lord has no doubt that the owners of the asses will acquiesce, if the disciples have need to make their imperious demand; He speaks as though it were not certain whether it would be necessary to make it. "If any man say unto you, Why do ye this? say ye that the Lord hath need of him; and straightway he will send him hither."[1] In the other case, our Lord's expression of relief and of delight on entering the Upper Chamber— "With desire I desired to eat this passover with you before I suffered"[2]—may perhaps be taken as a sign that He had not been wholly free from anxiety lest the preparations made secretly should be interrupted by the treachery of Judas.

There are many instances also of His supernatural knowledge of facts in the lives of men. He sees a poor widow casting two mites into the treasury; and with admiration and pleasure He summons His disciples to look at the woman —more worthy of attention than all those magnificent structures at which, a moment after, they in their turn ask Him to look. He tells them that her gift is more than that of all the rich men, for that she had "cast in everything that she had, even all her living."[3] Though occupied with His own trial before the High Priest, and probably out of earshot of what was taking place among the servants

[1] St. Matt. xxi. 3. [2] St. Luke xxii. 15. [3] St. Mark xii. 44.

ITS TRANSCENDENCE. 161

at the fire, the Lord's turn and the Lord's look showed that He was aware of St. Peter's fall, and understood his feelings.[1] St. John's Gospel adds four or five such examples. Christ sees Nathanael under the fig tree—not with the bodily eye—and discerns and discloses the subject of his meditations, and reads his character from them.[2] He unveils certain passages in the history of the Samaritan woman, in one pointed sentence, so accurately, that she says with little exaggeration, "He told me all things that ever I did."[3] He perceived, probably by a supernatural insight, that the impotent man at Bethesda had lain a long time in that case.[4] Far removed from the respective scenes, He announced to the disciples, "Lazarus is dead,"[5] and to the anxious courtier, "Thy son liveth."[6]

Several of the incidents already mentioned disclose a knowledge of things not only past and present, but also in the near future. Accordingly, we find our Lord not unfrequently elsewhere declaring particular events, external to

---

[1] St. Luke xxii. 61. [2] St. John i. 48. [3] St. John iv. 29.
[4] St. John v. 6. [5] St. John xi. 14. [6] St. John iv. 50.

His own life, before they occur. He foretells in detail the denial of St. Peter; He foretells, and has long foreseen, the treachery of Judas; He foresees every horror of the siege and of the destruction of Jerusalem. I do not class among these phenomena His utterance about Mary's anointing Him at Bethany[1] (which is often treated as an example of a prediction verified) because that was of the nature of a promise rather than a prophecy, and it was His saying that her action should be told which caused it to be told.

Before we go further, however, it is necessary to say—in view of criticisms that may be offered—that up to this point we have seen no supernatural knowledge in our Lord to which analogies may not be found in the lives of other men. Samuel tells Saul of the finding of his father's asses while at a distance, and predicts to him in detail the incidents of his journey home. Elisha, whose miraculous career in so many points resembles our Lord's, can tell, in the hyperbolical language of the Syrian

[1] St. Matt. xxvi. 13.

courtiers, the words which the king speaks in his bedchamber. His heart goes with Gehazi on his stealthy errand, and detects every movement in the transaction with Naaman. He announces beforehand the raising of the siege of Samaria, and the victories of Israel in the valley of Edom, and in Aphek. The blind Ahijah discerns the wife of Jeroboam before she knocks at his door. The secret sin of David is known to the prophet Nathan. There is no indication that I am aware of, that our Lord's supernatural knowledge in things of this nature differed in kind from that of the prophets; or from that of St. Peter, when he detected the sin of Ananias and Sapphira, or of St. Paul when he foretold the fortunes of the vessel on which he sailed, or of Agabus when he foretold the famine of Jerusalem and the binding of St. Paul's hands and feet. That our Lord's knowledge in such matters greatly exceeded that of others is evident; but we cannot say with certainty from the phenomena themselves that it came to Him in a different way from theirs, or that while they knew by spiritual revelation,

He knew by virtue of His own Divine omniscience. If there was such a difference, Holy Scripture does not make it, at any rate, salient.

We come upon somewhat different ground when we turn to our Lord's knowledge of facts in the moral order. It appears to be one thing to have a supernatural intimation (for instance) that Lazarus was dead, and another thing to discern the depths of character. It is hardly necessary to adduce examples, when the Gospels are full of them, of our Saviour's perfect insight into the moral state of those with whom He came in contact. It underlies the unwavering firmness of His direction of souls. "One thing thou lackest: go and sell all that thou hast, and give to the poor."[1] Unbelievers imagined that they had convicted Him of failure in this respect; and by so doing, gave occasion for displaying His insight in all its breadth and delicacy. "If this man were a prophet," they say—for they regarded such insight as part of the endowment of a prophet—"He would have known what manner of woman this is that toucheth

[1] St. Mark x. 21.

Him;"[1] and then follows the marvellous vindication of His discernment, both with regard to the woman and with regard to Simon the Pharisee himself.

And such discernment in the Lord Jesus is not the result of long personal intercourse and observation. It manifests itself at first meetings. It requires but a glance, and perhaps does not require even that. "Jesus looked upon him, and said, Thou art Simon the son of John; thou shalt be called Cephas, which is interpreted Peter."[2] "Jesus saw Nathanael coming to Him, and saith concerning him, Behold indeed an Israelite, in whom there is no guile."[3] Well might a man reply in surprise, "Whence knowest Thou me?" Everywhere there is the same unerring perception of character and of moral conditions. "I know you,"[4] He says to His enemies—though this is partly the knowledge of experience. "I know My sheep,"[5] He says of His friends. Quite at the outset of His work, St. John lays it down as a generalisation,

---

[1] St. Luke vii. 39.   [2] St. John i. 42.   [3] St. John i. 47.
[4] St. John v. 42: ἔγνωκα.   [5] St. John x. 14: γινώσκω.

to account for His reserve towards persons who gathered promisingly round Him. "Jesus did not entrust Himself to them, because He, for His part, knew all men, and inasmuch as He had no need that any one should give testimony concerning the man (that is, any given man with whom He was dealing) for He Himself always knew what was in the man," or possibly, "in man."[1] He read men's thoughts, moods, tendencies, inward conflicts, before they were expressed, before the men themselves were fully conscious of them; and on every page of the Gospels, His questions and His actions laid bare the secret things of other men's souls. It was not strange that those who lived consecutively with Him came to the conclusion that He knew, not only all men, but all things. "Now we know that Thou knowest all things, and needest not that any should question Thee."[2] "Lord, Thou knowest all things; Thou art aware that I love Thee."[3] And, at any rate,

---

[1] St. John ii. 24 foll.: διὰ τὸ αὐτὸν γινώσκειν πάντας ... αὐτὸς γὰρ ἐγίνωσκεν τί ἦν ἐν τῷ ἀνθρώπῳ).

[2] St. John xvi. 30: οἴδαμεν ὅτι οἶδας πάντα.

[3] St. John xxi. 17: πάντα σὺ οἶδας.

in the sense in which they meant it, the Lord Jesus did not disavow the ascription.

In this knowledge of men themselves, as distinguished from the knowledge of facts about them, our Lord is plainly without a rival. Discernment of character is a gift possessed by all men to some degree; by many, through the power of the Holy Ghost, in a high and supernatural degree; but no other has had the same penetration as Christ had. All others, we may well suppose, have made occasional mistakes about their men, but our Lord never did. His choice of a Judas into the number of the Twelve was not the result of ignorance, but of a long night of prayer, like the night in Gethsemane,[1] and a prelude to it. "I know whom I chose."[2]

As He was unrivalled in His penetration, so our Lord was unique in the range over which those powers of penetration were exercised. By what steps His knowledge of men extended, from the hour when He first began *risu cognoscere Matrem*, and knew no other face than hers, to the end of all, we are not told. But there

[1] St. Luke vi. 12.   [2] St. John xiii. 18.

seems to be reason to believe that when St. John says, "He knew all men," it does not mean only that He knew them when He met them. "Other sheep I have,"[1] He says; "Every one that is of the truth heareth My voice,"[2] as if He were conscious of spiritual relations already established between them and Him, although the time for mutual recognition and open government was not yet come. Saul of Tarsus and the Lord Jesus never met face to face during the Lord's earthly life; yet St. Paul says, "He loved me, and gave Himself for me."[3] It would seem an unwarranted impoverishment of the Apostle's language to explain that our Lord gave Himself for all men, and therefore, by implication, for St. Paul. We seem to be intended to gather that, at the close, at any rate, our Lord's horizon became actually coextensive with all whose nature was summed up in Him and whose sins He was to bear, and that each individual "brother" of His, however distant in time and clime, not only has a place in His thought and affection now, but

[1] St. John x. 16. [2] St. John xviii. 37. [3] Gal. ii. 20.

had a place in His thought and affection then. That from the Cross He actually commanded the whole field of human history, and came into conscious contact with every one of us, is a belief which St. Paul's language commends. Christ is in His human nature the very Head of that Body of which we are all members; and as, in His physical frame, He "could tell all His bones," each contributing its separate quotum to that sum of pain which He felt, so it may have been in His mystical body also, and while He bore "the sin of the world" as a vast whole, there may have been a power to discriminate the items also, and those by whose fault He came to bear them.

We advance now from the moral order to the Divine. Here we are on the surest ground. Our Lord's knowledge in Divine things is absolute and exhaustive.

It is so with regard to God Himself. No shadow of misgiving passes across His mind as He speaks of God. The holiest and wisest men have always felt most the danger of speaking of the Divine nature, knowing it to be infinitely above and beyond them. They have dreaded to be presumptuous and irreverent, to define rashly in a sphere of which they possess no positive knowledge. No saint who ever lived upon earth was more reverent than Christ. His prayers, we are told, were heard "by reason of His cautious reverence,"[1] and it is said of Him, as the climax of the Spirit's gifts, that He should be filled with the Spirit of the fear of the Lord.[2] His language about God and to God is that of the most solemn adoration. Yet He speaks of God as of one whom He knows and understands to the very depth, and of whom He, and He alone, is qualified to speak. "All things were delivered to Me by My Father, and none knoweth (ἐπιγινώσκει) the Son but the Father, neither doth any know the Father but the Son, and he to whomsoever the Son is pleased to reveal Him."[3] "Jesus cried in the temple, teaching and saying, Ye both know Me (οἴδατε), and ye know whence I am; and I am not come of Myself, but He is true that sent Me, whom

---

[1] Heb. v. 7: ἀπὸ τῆς εὐλαβείας.   [2] Isa. xi. 2, 3.
[3] St. Matt. xi. 27.

ye do not know. I know Him (οἶδα), because I am from Him, and He sent Me forth."¹ "If I glorify Myself, My glory is nothing; there is one who glorifieth Me, even My Father; of whom ye say that He is your God; and (all the while) ye have not known Him (ἐγνώκατε); but I know Him (οἶδα); and if I say that I do not know Him, I shall be, like you, a liar; but I know Him, and His word I keep."² "I am the Good Shepherd, and know My sheep, and am known of Mine, as the Father knoweth Me, and I know (γινώσκω) the Father."³

And as He knows the eternal Father, so also He knows the Holy Ghost. With entire confidence He opens out the mystery of the Holy Ghost's existence, and personality, and function, and connexion with the Father and Himself, which were unknown to men before. I need not quote the passages, which will readily come to mind; and some of them we shall need to mention by-and-by for another purpose.

The same intimate knowledge extends to all the unseen things, which are mysteries hidden

---

[1] St. John vii. 28 foll.   [2] St. John viii. 54.   [3] St. John x. 14.

from the eyes of the world. Not to refer to all our Saviour's teaching about heaven and hell, and the powers of the invisible order, it will be enough to refer to His own absolute claim to expound heavenly things,—although He deigns to associate others with Himself, as having experienced, through faith in Him, something of that of which He speaks. "Verily, verily, I say unto you"—to Nicodemus and his class—"that which we know (οἴδαμεν), we speak, and that which we have seen, we testify, and our testimony ye receive not. If I told you things on earth, and ye believe not, how shall ye believe if I tell you things in heaven?"[1]

But it is with regard to His own person and significance to the world that our Lord's witness is, for our present purpose, the most noteworthy. Some modern writers upon New Testament theology, such as Beyschlag, venture to speak of our Lord as manifesting "a purely human consciousness of Himself."[2] Such a theory, of course, presupposes the rejection of

---

[1] St. John iii. 11 foll.
[2] Beyschlag's *New Test. Theology* (Eng. transl.) i. 73.

ITS TRANSCENDENCE. 173

St. John's Gospel as a historical account of our Lord's teaching; but there are utterances enough in the Synoptic Gospels also to make the theory untenable.

Jesus had from early years known and laid to heart, in a way suitable to His tender age, His relationship to God. "Wist ye not," He says, at the age of twelve, "that I must be in My Father's house?"[1] We are not compelled to suppose that those gracious lips were prepared then and there to unfold, in the language of a later time, the whole mystery of His Person; but when He says, "My Father's," and not "God's," nor yet "Our Father's," we cannot but believe that in all grave simplicity He had felt within Himself a peculiar bond of kinship with Him whose the temple was. When once His ministry was begun, although He would not put the sublime conclusion ready-made in the mouths of men, He was perpetually engaged in teaching them the premisses that should lead to the conclusion that He was God,—though not for His own

[1] St. Luke ii. 49.

glorification, but that, believing Him to be what He was, they might recognise the character and purposes of the Father from whom He came. Such deep wells of self-revelation lie everywhere in St. John's Gospel; but they lie to a less extent in the others also.

Is it a purely human consciousness that is manifested, I will not say in the Sermon on the Mount, when Christ contrasts His new law, promulgated upon His own authority—"I say unto you,"—with all that had gone before; but in that threefold comparison contained in the twelfth chapter of St. Matthew: "I say unto you that something greater than the temple is here (τοῦ ἱεροῦ μεῖζον);"[1] "and lo, something more than Jonas is here (πλεῖον Ἰωνᾶ);"[2] "something more than Solomon is here (πλεῖον Σολομῶνος)?"[3] He does not compare Himself with Solomon or Jonas as a greater man than they were; that would have been πλείων or μείζων Σολομῶνος, πλείων Ἰωνᾶ. His greatness is not in the same order as theirs. There is a difference in their very essence.

[1] St. Matt. xii. 6.   [2] St. Matt. xii. 41.   [3] St. Matt. xii. 42.

The Jews at Jerusalem early caught and correctly interpreted His meaning, when, upon His saying, "My Father worketh hitherto, and I work," they inferred that He "claimed God in a special sense as His own Father (πατέρα ἴδιον ἔλεγε τὸν Θεόν), making Himself equal to God."[1] So He did indeed. When at a later period they again accused Him of "making Himself a God,"[2] instead of repudiating the alleged blasphemy, He showed them from the Scriptures that if a mere reception of Divine revelation gave to the recipients a right to the title of gods, His own unique office as the agent of revelation fully justified the claims which He had actually made. And those claims involved a co-equal Godhead with the Father. "I and the Father are one."[3] "Have I been so long time with you, and yet hast thou not known Me, Philip? He that hath seen Me, hath seen the Father. How sayest thou, Show us the Father?"[4] "Verily, verily, I say unto you, The Son cannot do anything of Himself, except He

---

[1] St. John v. 18.
[2] St. John x. 33.
[3] St. John x. 30.
[4] St. John xiv. 9.

behold the Father doing aught; for whatsoever He doeth, these things doeth the Son in like manner. For the Father loveth the Son, and showeth to Him all things that Himself doeth."[1] "The Father hath committed the whole judgment unto the Son, that all may honour the Son even as they honour the Father."[2] "The Spirit of truth shall guide you into all the truth; for He shall not speak from Himself, but as many things as He heareth, He shall speak . . . He shall glorify Me; because He shall take out of that which is Mine, and declare it unto you. All things whatsoever the Father hath are Mine; for this cause I said that He taketh out of that which is Mine, and shall declare it unto you."[3]

No words could more fully describe the Godhead of the Son according to its contents—if I may use the expression—than such texts as these. There can be no question but that Christ upon earth was fully conscious of His Divine essence; and when at last a great disciple sprang at a bound out of the depth of hopelessness

---

[1] St. John v. 19. [2] St. John v. 22.
[3] St. John xvi. 13 foll.

to the glorious confession, never made before, that Christ was his God, Jesus calmly accepted the adoration. While Peter, in the Acts, says with blunt simplicity to the prostrate Cornelius, "Stand up; I myself also am a man;" while twice over in the Apocalypse the interpreting angel, at whose feet the seer had fallen, cries in horror, "See thou do it not; I am thy fellow-servant;" while Jesus Himself abruptly rejects earthly honours that were not His: "Man, who made Me a judge or a divider over you?"[1] Jesus has no rebuke for St. Thomas's gesture and word of worship, save a gentle rebuke that it had not come sooner.[2]

Our Lord was not only fully conscious of His personal Godhead and oneness of essence with the Father. He was conscious of His former mode of existence, of His mission to the world, and of His uninterrupted connexion with God. The passages which bring these points before us sometimes bring more than one of them at a time, so that we may take them all together.

---

[1] St. Luke xii. 14. [2] St. John xx. 28.

That His former mode of existence was present to the mind of Jesus is shown, above all, in His last great prayer. "And now, O Father, glorify Thou Me beside Thyself, with the glory which I had, before the world was, beside Thee."[1] That glory is to Him a thing of the past and of the future, not of present enjoyment; but no oblivion puts it out of His remembrance. He speaks of those experiences of His life before the Incarnation in other passages where He is enforcing the authority of His mission. He desires, for instance, to tell Nicodemus of heavenly things, "And no one," He adds, "hath ascended into heaven, save He that came down out of heaven, even the Son of man."[2] Again He says, "Every one who hath heard from the Father, and learned, cometh to Me;—not that any hath seen the Father, except He who is from the side of God ($\dot{o}$ $\ddot{\omega}\nu$ $\pi\alpha\rho\grave{\alpha}$ $\tau o\hat{v}$ $\Theta\epsilon o\hat{v}$); He hath seen the Father."[3] The contrast

[1] St. John xvii. 5.
[2] St. John iii. 13. The words which follow in the Received Text, "which is in heaven," are no part of the original, and suggest a conception of Christ's life on earth which has no support in any other part of the Gospels.
[3] St. John v. 45 foll.

is again drawn: "Ye have never yet heard voice nor seen shape of Him, and His word ye have not abiding in you; because whom He sent, Him ye believe not."[1] Once more: "If I bear witness concerning Myself, My witness is true, because I know whence I came, and whither I go."[2]

But the connexion with the Father is no mere reminiscence of a great past. Again and again our Lord asseverates that the Father is and dwells "in" Him, and He "in" the Father. Although the Father has sent Him forth into the world, He has not broken off an active correspondence with Him, though it is maintained under a new form. "He that sent was still with Him that was sent." "He that sent Me is with Me. He did not leave Me alone, because I do always the things which please Him."[3] "If I judge, My judgment is true, because I am not alone; but I and the Father who sent Me."[4]

Sometimes, however, the mighty recollection

---

[1] St. John v. 37.
[2] St. John viii. 14.
[3] St. John viii. 29.
[4] St. John viii. 16.

of that "sanctification" and "sealing" which preceded His being "sent into the world" so dominates the mind of the Incarnate Lord, that He speaks as if all His teaching were based upon it, and as if a body of sacred truth had been once for all entrusted to Him, to be delivered in detail to men. "My doctrine is not Mine, but His that sent Me."[1] "He that sent Me is true; and *I* speak into the world what I heard from Him."[2] "The things which I have seen with the Father, I speak."[3] "Of Myself I do nothing, but according as the Father taught Me, I speak these things."[4] The heavenly instruction descends even to the successive details of the teaching. "I did not speak out of Myself"—so our Saviour finally looks back upon His concluded ministry of teaching—"but the Father who sent Me, Himself hath given Me a commandment, what I should say (in general), and what I should speak (in the particular form of the moment). . . . The things therefore which I speak,

[1] St. John vii. 16.
[2] St. John viii. 26.
[3] St. John viii. 38
[4] St. John viii. 28.

according as the Father hath said to Me, I so speak."[1]

And as it is with our Lord's teaching, so it is also with His action. He speaks of it sometimes as if imposed upon Him once for all in His original mission. This seems to be the purpose of all those sayings where He speaks of doing the will of Him that sent Him, or working the works of Him that sent Him. "According as the Father gave Me commandment, so I do."[2] "I glorified Thee upon the earth, by accomplishing the work which Thou hast given Me that I should do it."[3] St. John has been accused of making our Lord speak as if His life were the execution of a program; but the fact is so. He came, indeed, into the world with a program,—"In the volume of the book it is written of Me,"—and He consciously and conscientiously fulfilled it. There were no moments of vacillation in His life. Our Lord always moves straight towards His mark.

[1] St. John xii. 49 foll. [2] St. John xiv. 31.
[3] St. John xvii. 4.

It has often been observed how the sufferings of the Redeemer were enhanced by having been long foreknown to Him, even in minute particulars. The contemplation of them beforehand woke in Him a holy impatience to be in the midst of them. "I have a baptism to be baptized withal, and how am I straitened till it be accomplished!"[1] Doubtless, like other knowledge which He possessed, the knowledge of His appointed program of actions and of sufferings became ampler and more particular as time went on; but we can mention no date at which were first shown to Him the main outlines of what was in store for the Lamb of God. As far back as we can trace His thoughts —that is, from the Jordan and the Temptation onwards—He advances steadily in the direction of the Cross. At the first Passover after His ministry began, He already announces in a riddle His murder and His resurrection on the third day.[2] In His conversation of the same date with Nicodemus, He declares that He is to be lifted up like the Brazen Serpent in the

---

[1] St. Luke xii. 50. [2] St. John ii. 19.

wilderness.[1] As time goes on, He tells His disciples beforehand every hideous and revolting detail of the Trial and the Crucifixion. When it draws quite close, He calmly says, "Ye know that after two days is the Passover, and the Son of Man is betrayed to be crucified."[2] Nothing in that last dreadful chapter of His earthly history finds Him unprepared. At no period of His recorded life is there visible so tranquil and majestic a sense of being ready for all, and doing what had long been familiarised by mental rehearsal. "Before the feast of the Passover, Jesus knowing that His hour was come that He should depart out of this world unto the Father."[3] "Jesus, knowing all things that were coming upon Him, went forth."[4] "After this, Jesus knowing that all things were now finished, that the Scripture might be fulfilled, saith, I thirst."[5] Nor did Christ's acquaintance with His own program end here. He knew well beforehand, and had predicted, His resurrection and ascension, and in glorious

[1] St. John iii. 14. [2] St. Matt. xxvi. 2. [3] St. John xiii. 1.
[4] St. John xviii. 4. [5] St. John xix. 28.

fulness He predicted His return again to judge.

Our Lord had not only a complete and perfect knowledge of Himself and of His task; He knew also the preparation which the Divine Providence had made for His coming. The history set forth in the Bible was familiar to Him; and the teaching of lawgivers and prophets and wise men lay open to His mind. Our Saviour knew the Bible, though we are not told of His reading it, except in public. "How knoweth this Man letters (*i.e.* literary ways), having never learned (*i.e.* in the recognised schools of the teachers)?"[1] So men asked when they saw how much He knew. He found support for Himself in the Scriptures, in the wilderness of Temptation and on the Cross, and doubtless at other times. He affirmed without hesitation that He was Himself the chief theme of them. "Ye search the Scriptures, for in them *ye* think to have eternal life; and it is they that testify of Me; and yet ye will not come to Me that ye may have life."[2] "Think

---

[1] St. John vii. 16.   [2] St. John v. 39.

not that I will accuse you to the Father. There is one that accuseth you, even Moses, in whom ye have hoped. For if ye believed Moses, ye would have believed Me, for he wrote of Me."[1] "This that is written must yet be accomplished in Me."[2] "How then shall the Scriptures be fulfilled, that thus it must be?"[3] "Ye fools, and slow of heart to believe upon all that the prophets spake! Ought not the Christ to have suffered these things, and so to enter into His glory? And beginning at Moses and all the prophets, He expounded unto them in all the Scriptures the things concerning Himself."[4] "These are the words which I spake to you while I was yet with you, that all things written in the law of Moses and the Prophets and the Psalms concerning Me must be fulfilled. Then opened He their understanding that they might understand the Scriptures."[5] In every question respecting the interpretation of the Scriptures, our Lord moves with perfect freedom and

---

[1] St. John v. 45 foll.
[2] St. Luke xxii. 37.
[3] St. Matt. xxvi. 54.
[4] St. Luke xxiv. 25.
[5] St. Luke xxiv. 44 foll.

confidence, unhesitatingly. He knows their meaning and their value.

There is one very remarkable passage in St. John which seems to indicate that our Lord's knowledge of the Bible history was not all, at any rate, derived from the study of the Bible itself, or from any current interpretations of it. It is in the latter part of the eighth chapter, where the Jews accuse Jesus of making Himself greater than Abraham and the prophets, who were dead, while He professed to be able to give a deathless life. Jesus replied to the main charge, and then, to teach them the true relation between Abraham and Himself, He added, "Your father Abraham rejoiced to see My day; and He saw it, and was glad."[1] No incident is recorded in the Book of Genesis which directly affirms what our Lord affirmed, though there are recorded occasions to which such a blessed prevision of Christ's day may naturally be referred. The Jews, however, did not assail our Lord on the score of an interpretation; they assailed Him because His words seemed

[1] St. John viii. 56.

to imply some previous intercourse between Himself and the patriarch. They looked at the face and figure of the Man of thirty-three, worn and prematurely aged, as it appears, and said, "Thou are not yet fifty years old, and hast Thou seen Abraham? Jesus said unto them, Verily, verily, I say unto you, Before Abraham was, I am." Why did our Lord give this answer? Might He not have replied that He never said that He had seen Abraham, but that Abraham, in a sense, had seen Him? Might He not have said that His statement about Abraham was but a natural deduction from all that is told us in the Scriptures about the character of that holy man, and about the promises made to Him? But no; Jesus claimed, not indeed to have been alive on earth with Abraham, but to be above time altogether in His essential existence, and therefore to include the life of Abraham, and all history, within His experience and personal observation. He had indeed seen Abraham. He had witnessed the exultation with which Abraham caught sight, in the Spirit, of those far-off years when the promised Seed should come. He had witnessed it; and now, though incarnate, and Himself made subject to the laws of temporal existence, He had not forgotten the event. As, from His place on earth, He could look back and remember the glory which He had with the Father before His Incarnation, so, it seems, He could look back and remember how He had dealt with the heroes of the Old Testament hope, and had watched their spiritual progress.

A saying like this must make us careful of our words when we speak of our Saviour's human knowledge in relation to questions of Old Testament authorship and the like. He may well sometimes have used names like Moses and David in conventional senses; but Moses and David were real persons to Him, whom He had known, and had not forgotten. It is of interest to note how the New Testament writers speak of a special connexion between the person of the Blessed Lord and the development of the Old Testament history. When the Israelites ate and drank manna and miraculously given water in the wilderness, the food was "spiritual food," and "the rock was the Christ."[1] Moses himself "esteemed the reproach of the Christ greater riches than the treasures of Egypt."[2] The Spirit which inspired the prophets was "the Spirit of Christ in them."[3] All that pertained to the Holy Scriptures belonged to the personal history of the Divine Son, and seems to have come back to Him as such.

I have touched, though not with such completeness as I could wish, upon some of those departments in which our adorable Saviour's human knowledge transcended, to say the least of it, that of other men. There were, as we saw in my last lecture, points in which, though He made no mistake, He was contented not to know. But compare the kind of matters in which He seems to have not known, with those in which He knew! In infancy, doubtless, He knew but as an infant. In sleep, His knowledge of all that He knew was, like ours, in abeyance. In crises like the Agony, His hold upon what He knew—all but the one thing that was of

[1] 1 Cor. x. 4. [2] Heb. xi. 26. [3] 1 Peter i. 11.

immediate importance—seemed to be paralysed. But taking the normal waking hours of His last three years upon earth, the things which, according to the records, He appears to have not known are trivial facts, easily to be ascertained by an ordinary question, or by walking a few steps. The things which He knew were God and man, Himself and His saving work, the Bible and the Divine dispensations. Truly it concerns us little, as Christ never set Himself to speak on such topics, whether He ever turned His human attention upon facts of natural science or of secular history. All that it was profitable to know for His perfection and for our salvation, that we are assured that He knew with an accuracy and completeness in which there was no room for improvement.

This immeasurable wealth of human knowledge was derived, as we have seen, from various sources. First, there was His own observation—and His natural faculties were the most perfect that were ever created, and they had not been dulled by sin. Then for Him, as for us, there was the knowledge acquired by information from others. None can now tell how much was owing, under the Divine guidance, to the early instructions imparted by Mary, and by the good foster-father who taught Him a trade, and by doctors like those who clustered round Him in the Temple; only we may be sure that, when least intending it, His luminous and spiritual intelligence gave back a thousand times more (if only they had power to apprehend it) than what He gained from them. And then there was the enlightening grace of the Holy Ghost, by whose operation He first became flesh, and who found in the sacred youth of Jesus a perfect vessel for His use; and who, when the moment was come, descended upon Him, without measure, in all His entirety, opening all heaven to His sight, and keeping it ever open.

To that Holy Spirit's influence we may probably ascribe those kinds of special knowledge which (in a sense) were common to the Lord Jesus and to the prophets.[1] To His influence upon our

[1] "[The Scriptures] teach us that all His superhuman knowledge was supplied by the Father. . . . All things that the

Lord's unique humanity we may perhaps ascribe our Lord's penetration into the hearts and minds of men. To Him, the inspirer of the men of old, may perhaps be traced our Lord's perfect understanding of the Scriptures. It was by Him that, even after the Resurrection, Christ continued to give commandment to His disciples.[1] We saw, in the first lecture, that it was by Him that our Lord's miracles were wrought. Whether we are to go further still in the same direction is not made clear. It is possible that we are to believe that it was to the witness of the Holy Ghost that our Saviour upon earth owed His knowledge even of Himself, and of God, and of His connexion with God, and of His Sonship; that it was the Holy Ghost who brought to His inward as well as His outward ears the assurance, "Thou art My beloved Son, in whom I am

Omniscient Father knows,—that is, all things,—doubtless, were known to the Son, when He was 'in the form of God.' But it appears when He became Man, and dwelt among us, of this infinite knowledge He only possessed as much as was imparted to Him. And this being the case, we must see that, if anything which could not be known naturally was not made known to Him by the Father, it would not be known by Him" (Bishop O'Brien's *Charge* p. 110).

[1] Acts i. 2.

well pleased?" Thus, at last, even the knowledge of those things which our Blessed Saviour knew by virtue of His own unchanged personality—His wondrous remembrances brought with Him from afar—may have been due to the action of Him who brings all necessary things to the remembrance of the Christian, and whose great office in the eternal Godhead is to search the depths of the Divine self-consciousness, and to unite the Father with the Son.

It is possible that in the course of a difficult investigation I may sometimes have spoken in a way that has caused pain or perplexity to some of my hearers. If it be so, I would heartily ask their forbearance and forgiveness. I earnestly hope that I have not spoken without due reverence towards the Eternal Son of God, who is the subject of our thought; and I will beg all who have heard me to search the Scriptures candidly, like the noble Jews of Berœa, to see whether these things are so. Nothing is more to be desired than that we should go simply to our Bibles, and work at them afresh. These lectures will have a profitable result, if they set the students of this Seminary to read the Gospels with renewed interest, whether that study should issue in the establishing of the main suggestions which I have offered or in their refutation.

THE END.

www.ingramcontent.com/pod-product-compliance
Lightning Source LLC
Chambersburg PA
CBHW070739160426
43192CB00009B/1503